STRANGE STORIES
BY A NERVOUS GENTLEMAN

Washington Irving

STRANGE STORIES
BY A NERVOUS GENTLEMAN

by Washington Irving

APPLEWOOD BOOKS
Carlisle, Massachusetts

Part One from *Tales of a Traveller* by Washington Irving,
first published in 1824

978-1-4290-9538-9

CONTENTS.

STRANGE STORIES

BY

A NERVOUS GENTLEMAN.

I'll tell you more: there was a fish taken,
A monstrous fish, with a sword by 's side, a long sword,
A pike in 's neck, and a gun in 's nose, a huge gun,
And letters of mart in 's mouth from the Duke of Florence.
  Cleanthes. This is a monstrous lie.
  Tony.   I do confess it.
Do you think I'd tell you truths?
                                  FLETCHER'S *Wife for a Month.*

TO THE READER.

WORTHY AND DEAR READER ! — Hast thou ever been way-laid in the midst of a pleasant tour by some treacherous malady? thy heels tripped up, and thou left to count the tedious minutes as they passed, in the solitude of an inn chamber ? If thou hast, thou wilt be able to pity me. Behold me, interrupted in the course of my journeying up the fair banks of the Rhine, and laid up by indisposition in this old frontier town of Mentz.[1] I have worn out every source of amusement. I know the sound of every clock that strikes, and bell that rings, in the place. I know to a second when to listen for the first tap of the Prussian drum, as it summons the garrison to parade, or at what hour to expect the distant sound of the Austrian military band. All these have grown wearisome to me ; and even the well-known step of my doctor, as he slowly paces the corridor, with healing in the creak of his shoes, no longer affords an agreeable interruption to the monotony of my apartment.

For a time I attempted to beguile the weary hours by study-ing German under the tuition of mine host's pretty little daugh-ter, Katrine ; but I soon found even German had not power to charm a languid ear, and that the conjugating of *ich liebe*[2] might be powerless, however rosy the lips which uttered it.

I tried to read, but my mind would not fix itself. I turned over volume after volume, but threw them by with distaste. "Well, then," said I at length, in despair, "if I cannot read a book, I will write one." Never was there a more lucky idea ; it

[1] A city of Germany, the capital of Rhenish Hesse, situated on the left bank of the Rhine. It is a fortress, and has a garrison of eight hundred men.
[2] German for " I love."

at once gave me occupation and amusement. The writing of a book was considered in old times as an enterprise of toil and difficulty, insomuch that the most trifling lucubration was denominated a "work," and the world talked with awe and reverence of "the labors of the learned." These matters are better understood nowadays.

Thanks to the improvements in all kinds of manufactures, the art of bookmaking has been made familiar to the meanest capacity. Everybody is an author. The scribbling of a quarto is the mere pastime of the idle; the young gentleman throws off his brace of duodecimos in the intervals of the sporting season, and the young lady produces her set of volumes with the same facility that her great-grandmother worked a set of chair bottoms.

The idea having struck me, therefore, to write a book, the reader will easily perceive that the execution of it was no difficult matter. I rummaged my portfolio, and cast about in my recollection for those floating materials which a man naturally collects in traveling; and here I have arranged them in this little work.

As I know this to be a story-telling and a story-reading age, and that the world is fond of being taught by apologue, I have digested [1] the instruction I would convey into a number of tales. They may not possess the power of amusement which the tales told by many of my contemporaries possess; but then I value myself on the sound moral which each of them contains. This may not be apparent at first, but the reader will be sure to find it out in the end. I am for [2] curing the world by gentle alteratives, not by violent doses; indeed, the patient should never be conscious that he is taking a dose. I have learnt this much from experience under the hands of the worthy Hippocrates [3] of Mentz.

I am not, therefore, for those barefaced tales which carry their

---

[1] Distributed.   [2] "I am for," i.e., I am in favor of.
[3] A Greek physician (468–367 B.C.), called the "Father of Medicine;" hence, the doctor.

moral on the surface, staring one in the face; they are enough to deter the squeamish reader. On the contrary, I have often hid my moral from sight, and disguised it as much as possible by sweets and spices, so that while the simple reader is listening with open mouth to a ghost or a love story, he may have a bolus [1] of sound morality popped down his throat, and be never the wiser for the fraud.

As the public is apt to be curious about the sources whence an author draws his stories, doubtless that it may know how far to put faith in them, I would observe that the "Adventure of the German Student," or rather the latter part of it, is founded on an anecdote related to me as existing somewhere in French; and, indeed, I have been told, since writing it, that an ingenious tale has been founded on it by an English writer; but I have never met with either the former or the latter in print. Some of the circumstances in the "Adventure of the Mysterious Picture," and in "The Story of the Young Italian," are vague recollections of anecdotes related to me some years since; but from what source derived, I do not know. The adventure of the young painter among the banditti is taken almost entirely from an authentic narrative in manuscript.

As to the other tales contained in this work, and indeed to my tales generally, I can make but one observation: I am an old traveler, I have read somewhat, heard and seen more, and dreamt more than all. My brain is filled, therefore, with all kinds of odds and ends. In traveling, these heterogeneous matters have become shaken up in my mind, as the articles are apt to be in an ill-packed traveling trunk; so that when I attempt to draw forth a fact, I cannot determine whether I have read, heard, or dreamt it; and I am always at a loss to know how much to believe of my own stories.

These matters being premised, fall to,[2] worthy reader, with good appetite, and, above all, with good humor, to what is here set before thee. If the tales I have furnished should prove to

[1] A large pill.   [2] "Fall to," i.e., begin.

be bad, they will at least be found short; so that no one will be wearied long on the same theme. "Variety is charming," as some poet observes.

There is a certain relief in change, even though it be from bad to worse! As I have often found in traveling in a stagecoach, that it is often a comfort to shift one's position, and be bruised in a new place.

Ever thine,
GEOFFREY CRAYON.[1]

Dated from the HOTEL DE DARMSTADT,
   ci-divant[2] HOTEL DE PARIS,
  MENTZ, *otherwise called* MAYENCE.

THE GREAT UNKNOWN.

THE following adventures were related to me by the same nervous gentleman who told me the romantic tale of "The Stout Gentleman,"[3] published in "Bracebridge Hall." It is very singular that, although I expressly stated that story to have been told to me, and described the very person who told it, still it has been received as an adventure that happened to myself. Now I protest I never met with any adventure of the kind. I should not have grieved at this, had it not been intimated by the author of "Waverley," in an introduction to his novel of "Peveril of the Peak," that he was himself the stout gentleman alluded to. I have ever since been importuned by questions and letters from

---

[1] Washington Irving's pen name.   [2] Formerly.

[3] The Stout Gentleman is the name of one of Irving's most humorous sketches. The nervous gentleman above referred to amuses himself on a rainy Sunday in a country inn by conjectures as to the personality and character of an unknown "stout gentleman," who remains during the day shut up in a room in the inn. After greatly arousing the curiosity of the reader, the nervous gentleman manages just to get a glimpse of the rear of a person getting into a stagecoach, which was all he ever saw of the stout gentleman.

gentlemen, and particularly from ladies without number, touching what I had seen of the "Great Unknown."[1]

Now all this is extremely tantalizing. It is like being congratulated on the high prize when one has drawn a blank;[2] for I have just as great a desire as any one of the public to penetrate the mystery of that very singular personage, whose voice fills every corner of the world, without any one being able to tell whence it comes.

My friend the nervous gentleman, also, who is a man of very shy, retired habits, complains that he has been excessively annoyed in consequence of its getting about in his neighborhood that he is the fortunate personage; insomuch, that he has become a character of considerable notoriety in two or three country towns, and has been repeatedly teased to exhibit himself at bluestocking[3] parties, for no other reason than that of being "the gentleman who has had a glimpse of the author of 'Waverley.'"

Indeed, the poor man has grown ten times as nervous as ever since he has discovered, on such good authority, who the stout gentleman was; and will never forgive himself for not having made a more resolute effort to get a full sight of him. He has anxiously endeavored to call up a recollection of what he saw of that portly personage; and has ever since kept a curious eye on all gentlemen of more than ordinary dimensions, whom he has seen getting into stagecoaches. All in vain ! The features he had caught a glimpse of seem common to the whole race of stout gentlemen, and the " Great Unknown " remains as great an unknown as ever.

---

[1] Sir Walter Scott (1771–1832), Scottish novelist and poet, author of the Waverley Novels. Some of Scott's novels were published anonymously, and their author was called the " Great Unknown."

[2] A ticket in a lottery, on which no prize is indicated.

[3] A term applied to literary ladies. The name is derived from Mr. Stillingfleet, who was an indispensable attendant at certain meetings held in the eighteenth century by English ladies, for conversation with literary men, and who always wore blue stockings. Hence the names " bluestocking clubs " and " bluestockings."

Having premised these circumstances, I will now let the nervous gentleman proceed with his stories.

THE HUNTING DINNER.

I WAS once at a hunting dinner, given by a worthy fox-hunting old Baronet, who kept bachelor's hall in jovial style in an ancient, rook-haunted family mansion, in one of the middle counties. He had been a devoted admirer of the fair sex in his younger days; but, having traveled much, studied the sex in various countries with distinguished success, and returned home profoundly instructed, as he supposed, in the ways of woman, and a perfect master of the art of pleasing, he had the mortification of being jilted by a little boarding-school girl, who was scarcely versed in the accidence [1] of love.

The Baronet was completely overcome by such an incredible defeat; retired from the world in disgust; put himself under the government of his housekeeper; and took to fox hunting like a perfect Nimrod.[2] Whatever poets may say to the contrary, a man will grow out of love as he grows old; and a pack of fox hounds may chase out of his heart even the memory of a boarding-school goddess. The Baronet was, when I saw him, as merry and mellow an old bachelor as ever followed a hound; and the love he had once felt for one woman had spread itself over the whole sex, so that there was not a pretty face in the whole country round but came in for a share.

The dinner was prolonged till a late hour; for our host having no ladies in his household to summon us to the drawing-room, the bottle maintained its true bachelor sway, unrivaled by its potent enemy, the teakettle. The old hall in which we dined

[1] Conjugation.

[2] " A mighty hunter before the Lord " (see Gen. x. 8–12). The traditional notion of his character connects with it ideas of violence and insolence.

echoed to bursts of robustious [1] fox-hunting merriment, that made the ancient antlers shake on the walls. By degrees, however, the wine and the wassail of mine host began to operate upon bodies. already a little jaded by the chase. The choice spirits which flashed up at the beginning of the dinner sparkled for a time, then gradually went out one after another, or only emitted now and then a faint gleam from the socket. Some of the briskest talkers, who had given tongue so bravely at the first burst,[2] fell fast asleep; and none kept on their way but certain of those long-winded prosers, who, like short-legged hounds, worry on unnoticed at the bottom [3] of conversation, but are sure to be in at the death.[4] Even these at length subsided into silence; and scarcely anything was heard but the nasal communications of two or three veteran masticators, who, having been silent while awake, were indemnifying the company in their sleep.

At length the announcement of tea and coffee in the cedar parlor roused all hands from this temporary torpor. Every one awoke marvelously renovated, and while sipping the refreshing beverage out of the Baronet's old-fashioned hereditary china, began to think of departing for their several homes. But here a sudden difficulty arose. While we had been prolonging our repast, a heavy winter storm had set in, with snow, rain, and sleet, driven by such bitter blasts of wind that they threatened to penetrate to the very bone.

"It's all in vain," said our hospitable host, "to think of putting one's head out of doors in such weather. So, gentlemen, I hold you my guests for this night at least, and will have your quarters prepared accordingly."

The unruly weather, which became more and more tempestu-

---

[1] Hearty.

[2] "Had given tongue," etc., i.e., had talked so well in the beginning.

[3] Beginning.

[4] "In at the death," a term used in fox hunting, meaning to come up with the game before it has been killed by the hounds; hence, to be present at the end of anything.

ous, rendered the hospitable suggestion unanswerable. The only question was whether such an unexpected accession of company to an already crowded house would not put the housekeeper to her trumps [1] to accommodate them.

"Pshaw!" cried mine host; "did you ever know a bachelor's hall that was not elastic, and able to accommodate twice as many as it could hold?"

So, out of a good-humored pique, the housekeeper was summoned to a consultation before us all. The old lady appeared in her gala suit of faded brocade, which rustled with flurry and agitation; for, in spite of our host's bravado, she was a little perplexed. But in a bachelor's house, and with bachelor guests, these matters are readily managed. There is no lady of the house to stand upon squeamish points about lodging gentlemen in odd holes and corners, and exposing the shabby parts of the establishment. A bachelor's housekeeper is used to shifts and emergencies; so, after much worrying to and fro. and divers consultations about the red room, and the blue room, and the chintz room, and the damask room, and the little room with the bow window, the matter was finally arranged.

When all this was done, we were once more summoned to the standing rural amusement of eating. The time that had been consumed in dozing after dinner, and in the refreshment and consultation of the cedar parlor, was sufficient, in the opinion of the rosy-faced butler, to engender a reasonable appetite for supper. A slight repast had therefore been tricked [2] up from the residue of dinner, consisting of a cold sirloin of beef, hashed venison, a deviled leg of a turkey or so, and a few other of those light articles taken by country gentlemen to insure sound sleep and heavy snoring.

The nap after dinner had brightened up every one's wit; and a great deal of excellent humor was expended upon the perplexities of mine host and his housekeeper, by certain married gentlemen of the company, who considered themselves privileged in

---

[1] "Put to her trumps," i.e., test all her ingenuity.   [2] Served.

joking with a bachelor's establishment. From this the banter turned as to what quarters each would find, on being thus suddenly billeted in so antiquated a mansion.

"By my soul," said an Irish captain of dragoons, one of the most merry and boisterous of the party, "by my soul, but I should not be surprised if some of those good-looking gentlefolks that hang along the walls should walk about the rooms of this stormy night; or if I should find the ghost of one of those long-waisted ladies turning into my bed in mistake for her grave in the churchyard."

"Do you believe in ghosts, then?" said a thin, hatchet-faced [1] gentleman, with projecting eyes like a lobster.

I had remarked this last personage during dinner time for one of those incessant questioners, who have a craving, unhealthy appetite in conversation. He never seemed satisfied with the whole of a story; never laughed when others laughed; but always put the joke to the question. He never could enjoy the kernel of the nut, but pestered himself to get more out of the shell. "Do you believe in ghosts, then?" said the inquisitive gentleman.

"Faith, but I do," replied the jovial Irishman. "I was brought up in the fear and belief of them. We had a Benshee in our own family, honey."

"A Benshee — and what's that?" cried the questioner.

"Why, an old lady ghost that tends upon your real Milesian [2] families, and waits at their window to let them know when some of them are to die."

"A mighty pleasant piece of information!" cried an elderly gentleman with a knowing look, and with a flexible nose to which he could give a whimsical twist when he wished to be waggish.

"By my soul, but I'd have you to know it's a piece of distinction to be waited on by a Benshee. It's a proof that one has pure blood in one's veins. But i' faith, now we are talking of

---

[1] With a face like the edge of a hatchet; hence, sharp-faced.
[2] Irish.

ghosts, there never was a house or a night better fitted than the present for a ghost adventure. Pray, Sir John, haven't you such a thing as a haunted chamber to put a guest in ? "

"Perhaps," said the Baronet, smiling, "I might accommodate you even on that point."

"Oh, I should like it of all things, my jewel.[1] Some dark oaken room, with ugly, woe-begone portraits, that stare dismally at one, and about which the housekeeper has a power of [2] delightful stories of love and murder. And then a dim lamp, a table with a rusty sword across it, and a specter all in white, to draw aside one's curtains at midnight " —

"In truth," said an old gentleman at one end of the table, "you put me in mind of an anecdote " —

"Oh, a ghost story ! a ghost story !" was vociferated round the board, every one edging his chair a little nearer.

The attention of the whole company was now turned upon the speaker. He was an old gentleman, one side of whose face was no match for the other. The eyelid drooped and hung down like an unhinged window shutter; indeed, the whole side of his head was dilapidated, and seemed like the wing of a house shut up and haunted. I'll warrant that side was well stuffed with ghost stories.

There was a universal demand for the tale.

"Nay," said the old gentleman, "it's a mere anecdote, and a very commonplace one ; but such as it is you shall have it. It is a story that I once heard my uncle tell as having happened to himself. He was a man very apt to meet with strange adventures. I have heard him tell of others much more singular."

"What kind of a man was your uncle ? " said the questioning gentleman.

"Why, he was rather a dry, shrewd kind of body ; a great traveler, and fond of telling his adventures."

"Pray, how old might he have been when that happened ? "

---

[1] A term of endearment.
[2] "A power of," i.e., a great number of.

"When what happened ? " cried the gentleman with the flexible nose, impatiently. " Egad, you have not given anything a
chance to happen. Come, never mind our uncle's age; let us
have his adventures."

The inquisitive gentleman being for the moment silenced, the
old gentleman with the haunted head proceeded.

THE ADVENTURE OF MY UNCLE.

MANY years since, some time before the French Revolution,[1]
my uncle passed several months at Paris. The English
and French were on better terms in those days than at present,
and mingled cordially in society. The English went abroad to
spend money then, and the French were always ready to help
them. They go abroad to save money at present, and that they
can do without French assistance. Perhaps the traveling English were fewer and choicer than at present, when the whole
nation has broke[2] loose and inundated the continent. At any
rate, they circulated more readily and currently in foreign society,
and my uncle, during his residence in Paris, made many very intimate acquaintances among the French noblesse.[3]

Some time afterwards, he was making a journey in the winter
time in that part of Normandy called the Pays de Caux, when,
as evening was closing in, he perceived the turrets of an ancient
chateau rising out of the trees of its walled park ; each turret with
its high, conical roof of gray slate, like a candle with an extin-
guisher on it.

---

[1] The great French Revolution (1789–94), a tremendous upheaval of society, caused by the revolt of the people against the abuses of the higher classes,
and the despotism of the king. It resulted in the establishment of a democratic republic, followed by an empire resting on military power.

[2] Old form of " broken."   [3] Persons of noble rank.

"To whom does that chateau belong, friend?" cried my uncle to a meager but fiery postilion, who, with tremendous jack boots and cocked hat, was floundering on before him.

"To Monseigneur [1] the Marquis de ——," said the postilion, touching his hat, partly out of respect to my uncle, and partly out of reverence to the noble name pronounced.

My uncle recollected the Marquis for a particular friend in Paris, who had often expressed a wish to see him at his paternal chateau. My uncle was an old traveler, one who knew well how to turn things to account. He revolved for a few moments in his mind how agreeable it would be to his friend the Marquis to be surprised in this sociable way by a pop [2] visit; and how much more agreeable to himself to get into snug quarters in a chateau, and have a relish of the Marquis's well-known kitchen, and a smack of his superior champagne and Burgundy, rather than put up with the miserable lodgment and miserable fare of a provincial inn. In a few minutes, therefore, the meager postilion was cracking his whip like a very devil, or like a true Frenchman, up the long, straight avenue that led to the chateau.

You have no doubt all seen French chateaus, as everybody travels in France nowadays. This was one of the oldest, standing naked and alone in the midst of a desert of gravel walks and cold stone terraces, with a cold-looking, formal garden, cut into angles and rhomboids, and a cold, leafless park, divided geometrically by straight alleys, and two or three cold-looking, noseless statues; and fountains spouting cold water enough to make one's teeth chatter. At least such was the feeling they imparted on the wintry day of my uncle's visit; though, in hot summer weather, I'll warrant there was glare enough to scorch one's eyes out.

The smacking of the postilion's whip, which grew more and more intense the nearer they approached, frightened a flight of pigeons out of a dovecot, and rooks out of the roofs, and finally a crew of servants out of the chateau, with the Marquis at their

---

[1] A French title of rank.   [2] Unexpected.

head. He was enchanted to see my uncle, for his chateau, like the house of our worthy host, had not many more guests at the time than it could accommodate. So he kissed my uncle on each cheek, after the French fashion, and ushered him into the castle.

The Marquis did the honors of the house with the urbanity of his country. In fact, he was proud of his old family chateau, for part of it was extremely old. There was a tower and chapel which had been built almost before the memory of man ; but the rest was more modern, the castle having been nearly demolished during the wars of the league.[1] The Marquis dwelt upon this event with great satisfaction, and seemed really to entertain a grateful feeling towards Henry IV.[2] for having thought his paternal mansion worth battering down. He had many stories to tell of the prowess of his ancestors; and several skullcaps, helmets, and crossbows, and divers huge boots and buff jerkins, to show, which had been worn by the leaguers. Above all, there was a two-handed sword, which he could hardly wield, but which he displayed as a proof that there had been giants in his family.

In truth, he was but a small descendant from such great warriors. When you looked at their bluff visages and brawny limbs, as depicted in their portraits, and then at the little Marquis, with his spindleshanks[3] and his sallow lantern visage,[4] flanked with a pair of powdered earlocks, or *aîles de pigeon*,[5] that seemed ready to fly away with it, you could hardly believe him to be of the same race. But when you looked at the eyes that sparkled out like a beetle's from each side of his hooked nose, you saw at once that he inherited all the fiery spirit of his forefathers. In

1 " Wars of the league," i.e., civil wars in France (1562–98), caused originally by the enmity between the Catholics and the Huguenots, but developing later into a purely political strife in which most of the nations of Europe took part.

2 Henry IV. (1553–1610), King of France and Navarre, the first of the House of Bourbon.

3 Slender legs.   4 " Lantern visage," i.e., long, thin face.

5 Curls of hair near the ears ; literally, pigeon wings.

fact, a Frenchman's spirit never exhales, however his body may dwindle. It rather rarefies, and grows more inflammable, as the earthly particles diminish; and I have seen valor enough in a little fiery-hearted French dwarf to have furnished out a tolerable giant.

When once the Marquis, as was his wont, put on one of the old helmets stuck up in his hall, though his head no more filled it than a dry pea its peascod, yet his eyes flashed from the bottom of the iron cavern with the brilliancy of carbuncles; and when he poised the ponderous two-handed sword of his ancestors, you would have thought you saw the doughty little David wielding the sword of Goliath,[1] which was unto him like a weaver's beam.

However, gentlemen, I am dwelling too long on this description of the Marquis and his chateau, but you must excuse me; he was an old friend of my uncle, and whenever my uncle told the story, he was always fond of talking a great deal about his host. Poor little Marquis! He was one of that handful of gallant courtiers who made such a devoted but hopeless stand in the cause of their sovereign, in the chateau of the Tuileries,[2] against the irruption of the mob on the sad 10th of August. He displayed the valor of a preux[3] French chevalier to the last; flourishing feebly his little court sword with a *ça-ça!*[4] in face of a whole legion of *sans-culottes;*[5] but was pinned to the wall like

---

[1] A giant leader of the Philistines, supposed to have flourished in the eleventh century B.C. He challenged the Israelites to single combat, but no one was found willing to meet him except David (Hebrew poet, prophet, and king, born about 1090 B.C.), who slew him with a stone from his sling (see 1 Sam. xvii).

[2] During the French Revolution, Louis XVI., King of France, took up his abode in the palace of the Tuileries in Paris. On Aug. 10, 1792, a mob, armed with weapons of every sort, rushed upon the Tuileries, battering its walls and destroying everything within reach. The King escaped, but was shortly after imprisoned, and executed in 1793.

[3] Brave.   [4] A French exclamation; literally, " so, so."

[5] *Sans-culottes* (" ragamuffins ") was a name applied in contempt to the

a butterfly, by the pike of a *poissarde*,[1] and his heroic soul was borne up to heaven on his *ailes de pigeon.*

But all this has nothing to do with my stoŕy. To the point, then. When the hour arrived for retiring for the night, my uncle was shown to his room in a venerable old tower. It was the oldest part of the chateau, and had in ancient times been the donjon or stronghold; of course the chamber was none of the best. The Marquis had put him there, however, because he knew him to be a traveler of taste, and fond of antiquities; and also because the better apartments were already occupied. Indeed, he perfectly reconciled my uncle to his quarters by mentioning the great personages who had once inhabited them, all of whom were, in some way or other, connected with the family. If you would take his word for it, John Baliol, or, as he called him, Jean de Bailleul, had died of chagrin in this very chamber, on hearing of the success of his rival, Robert de Bruce, at the battle of Bannockburn; [2] and when he added that the Duke de Guise [3] had slept in it, my uncle was fain to felicitate himself on being honored with such distinguished quarters.

democrats of the French Revolution, who were styled the "ragamuffins of society." They, however, glorying in the name, affected a negligence of dress, and went about in blouses, red caps, and wooden shoes.

[1] A woman of the lowest class.

[2] Towards the end of the thirteenth century a great feud arose in Scotland over the succession to the throne. The chief claimants were Robert Bruce (1210–95) and John Baliol (1249–1315). Edward I. of England, claiming the right of decision, handed the government over to Baliol, subject to his command. After a while, however, the Scots, desiring perfect freedom, rebelled, with Baliol as their leader. The English conquered, Baliol resigned and was taken prisoner, and the King of England ruled Scotland through a council of regency till 1305. Then Scotland again sprang to arms under Robert Bruce (1274–1329), grandson of the original claimant. The English were badly defeated in the battle of Bannockburn, June 24, 1314, and the Scotch independence was regained, though not formally recognized by England till 1328.

[3] There are several men famous in French history who bear the name of "Duke de Guise." This probably refers to Henry I. of Lorraine (1550–88),

3

The night was shrewd [1] and windy, and the chamber none of the warmest. An old, long-faced, long-bodied servant, in quaint livery, who attended upon my uncle, threw down an armful of wood beside the fireplace, gave a queer look about the room, and then wished him *bon repos*,[2] with a grimace and a shrug that would have been suspicious from any other than an old French servant.

The chamber had indeed a wild, crazy look, enough to strike any one who had read romances with apprehension and foreboding. The windows were high and narrow, and had once been loopholes, but had been rudely enlarged, as well as the extreme thickness of the walls would permit; and the ill-fitted casements rattled to every breeze. You would have thought, on a windy night, some of the old leaguers were tramping and clanking about the apartment in their huge boots and rattling spurs. A door which stood ajar, and, like a true French door, would stand ajar in spite of every reason and effort to the contrary, opened upon a long, dark corridor, that led the Lord knows whither, and seemed just made for ghosts to air themselves in, when they turned out of their graves at midnight. The wind would spring up into a hoarse murmur through this passage, and creak the door to and fro, as if some dubious ghost were balancing in its mind whether to come in or not. In a word, it was precisely the kind of comfortless apartment that a ghost, if ghost there were in the chateau, would single out for its favorite lounge.

My uncle, however, though a man accustomed to meet with strange adventures, apprehended none at the time. He made several attempts to shut the door, but in vain. Not that he apprehended anything, for he was too old a traveler to be daunted by a wild-looking apartment; but the night, as I have said, was cold and gusty, and the wind howled about the old turret pretty much as it does round this old mansion at this moment,

Duke de Guise, surnamed "Balafré the Scarred," on account of a wound received in battle.

1 Keen.   2 Good night.

and the breeze from the long dark corridor came in as damp and as chilly as if from a dungeon. My uncle, therefore, since he could not close the door, threw a quantity of wood on the fire, which soon sent up a flame in the great wide-mouthed chimney that illumined the whole chamber, and made the shadow of the tongs on the opposite wall look like a long-legged giant. My uncle now clambered on the top of the half score of mattresses which form a French bed, and which stood in a deep recess; then, tucking himself snugly in, and burying himself up to the chin in the bedclothes, he lay looking at the fire, and listening to the wind, and thinking how knowingly he had come over his friend the Marquis for a night's lodging—and so he fell asleep.

He had not taken above half of his first nap when he was awakened by the clock of the chateau, in the turret over his chamber, which struck midnight. It was just such an old clock as ghosts are fond of. It had a deep, dismal tone, and struck so slowly and tediously that my uncle thought it would never have done. He counted and counted till he was confident he counted thirteen, and then it stopped.

The fire had burned low, and the blaze of the last fagot was almost expiring, burning in small blue flames, which now and then lengthened up into little white gleams. My uncle lay with his eyes half closed, and his nightcap drawn almost down to his nose. His fancy was already wandering, and began to mingle up the present scene with the crater of Vesuvius, the French Opera, the Coliseum [1] at Rome, Dolly's chophouse in London, and all the farrago of noted places with which the brain of a traveler is crammed,—in a word, he was just falling asleep.

Suddenly he was roused by the sound of footsteps, slowly pacing along the corridor. My uncle, as I have often heard him say himself, was a man not easily frightened. So he lay quiet,

---

[1] A large Roman amphitheater, one of the most imposing structures in the world, finished in A.D. 80. When first built it was chiefly used for the combats of the gladiators. It is now in ruins.

supposing this some other guest, or some servant on his way to bed. The footsteps, however, approached the door; the door gently opened, — whether of its own accord, or whether pushed open, my uncle could not distinguish; a figure all in white glided in. It was a female, tall and stately, and of a commanding air. Her dress was of an ancient fashion, ample in volume, and sweeping the floor. She walked up to the fireplace, without regarding my uncle, who raised his nightcap with one hand, and stared earnestly at her. She remained for some time standing by the fire, which, flashing up at intervals, cast blue and white gleams of light, that enabled my uncle to remark her appearance minutely.

Her face was ghastly pale, and perhaps rendered still more so by the bluish light of the fire. It possessed beauty, but its beauty was saddened by care and anxiety. There was the look of one accustomed to trouble, but of one whom trouble could not cast down nor subdue; for there was still the predominating air of proud, unconquerable resolution. Such, at least, was the opinion formed by my uncle, and he considered himself a great physiognomist.

The figure remained, as I said, for some time by the fire, putting out first one hand, then the other; then each foot alternately, as if warming itself; for your ghosts, if ghost it really was, are apt to be cold. My uncle, furthermore, remarked that it wore high-heeled shoes, after an ancient fashion, with paste or diamond buckles that sparkled as though they were alive. At length the figure turned gently round, casting a glassy look about the apartment, which, as it passed over my uncle, made his blood run cold, and chilled the very marrow in his bones. It then stretched its arms towards heaven, clasped its hands, and wringing them in a supplicating manner, glided slowly out of the room.

My uncle lay for some time meditating on this visitation, for (as he remarked when he told me the story), though a man of firmness, he was also a man of reflection, and did not reject a thing because it was out of the regular course of events. However, being, as I have before said, a great traveler, and accustomed to strange adventures, he drew his nightcap resolutely over his eyes, turned his back to the door, hoisted the bedclothes high over his shoulders, and gradually fell asleep.

How long he slept he could not say, when he was awakened by the voice of some one at his bedside. He turned round, and beheld the old French servant, with his earlocks in tight buckles on each side of a long, lantern face, on which habit had deeply wrinkled an everlasting smile. He made a thousand grimaces, and asked a thousand pardons for disturbing Monsieur, but the morning was considerable advanced. While my uncle was dressing, he called vaguely to mind the visitor of the preceding night. He asked the ancient domestic what lady was in the habit of rambling about this part of the chateau at night. The old valet shrugged his shoulders as high as his head, laid one hand on his bosom, threw open the other with every finger extended, made a most whimsical grimace which he meant to be complimentary, and replied that it was not for him to know anything of *les bonnes fortunes* [1] of Monsieur.

My uncle saw there was nothing satisfactory to be learned in this quarter. After breakfast, he was walking with the Marquis through the modern apartments of the chateau, sliding over the well-waxed floors of silken saloons, amidst furniture rich in gilding and brocade, until they came to a long picture gallery, containing many portraits, some in oil and some in chalks.

Here was an ample field for the eloquence of his host, who had all the pride of a nobleman of the *ancien régime*.[2] There was not a grand name in Normandy, and hardly one in France, which was not, in some way or other, connected with his house. My uncle stood listening with inward impatience, resting sometimes on one leg, sometimes on the other, as the little Marquis descanted, with his usual fire and vivacity, on the achievements of his ancestors, whose portraits hung along the wall; from the

[1] Adventures; literally, the good fortune.
[2] Ancient order of things, that obtained in France prior to the Revolution (see Note 1, p. 29).

martial deeds of the stern warriors in steel, to the gallantries and
intrigues of the blue-eyed gentlemen, with fair, smiling faces, powdered earlocks, laced ruffles, and pink and blue silk coats and
breeches; not forgetting the conquests of the lovely shepherdesses,
with hooped petticoats, and waists no thicker than an hourglass,
who appeared ruling over their sheep and their swains, with dainty
crooks decorated with fluttering ribbons.

In the midst of his friend's discourse, my uncle was startled
on beholding a full-length portrait, the very counterpart of his
visitor of the preceding night.

" Methinks," said he, pointing to it, " I have seen the original
of this portrait."

" *Pardonnez moi,*" [1] replied the Marquis politely, "that can
hardly be, as the lady has been dead more than a hundred years.
That was the beautiful Duchess de Longueville, who figured during the minority of Louis XIV."

" And was there anything remarkable in her history ? "

Never was question more unlucky. The little Marquis immediately threw himself into the attitude of a man about to tell a long
story. In fact, my uncle had pulled upon himself the whole history of the civil war of the Fronde,[2] in which the beautiful Duch-

1 Excuse me.

2 Louis XIV. (1638–1715) succeeded his father as King of France at the
age of five, but during his minority the management of the government was
virtually left to Cardinal Jules Mazarin (1602–61), who had succeeded Cardinal Richelieu as prime minister. The war of the Fronde was a rising of
the nobles to throw off the yoke laid on them by Richelieu, who had brought
them into subjection to the King. The immediate cause of the outbreak was
the attempt of Mazarin to punish the Parliament of Paris for having brought
about the dismissal of a favorite, but corrupt, agent of his. When Broussel,
a member especially beloved by the people, was arrested, the mob rose in
arms, seized whatever they could lay hands on, and barricaded the streets of
Paris, Aug. 5, 1648. Broussel being released, quiet was for a time restored.
Then it was that the discontented nobles united their cause with that of Paris
and the Parliament, and a new war of the Fronde broke out. The chief
instigator was the Duchess de Longueville (1619–79), daughter of Henri de
Bourbon, Prince de Condé. She induced her husband, the Duc de Longue-

ess had played so distinguished a part. Turenne, Coligni, Mazarin, were called up from their graves to grace his narration; nor
were the affairs of the barricaders nor the chivalry of the portes
cochères [1] forgotten. My uncle began to wish himself a thousand
leagues off from the Marquis and his merciless memory, when
suddenly the little man's recollections took a more interesting
turn. He was relating the imprisonment of the Duke de Longueville with the Princes Condé and Conti in the chateau of Vincennes,[2] and the ineffectual efforts of the Duchess to rouse the
sturdy Normans to their rescue. He had come to that part where
she was invested by the royal forces in the castle of Dieppe.[3]

"The spirit of the Duchess," proceeded the Marquis, "rose
from her trials. It was astonishing to see so delicate and beautiful a being buffet so resolutely with hardships. She determined
on a desperate means of escape. You may have seen the chateau
in which she was mewed up, — an old ragged wart of an edifice,
standing on the knuckle of a hill, just above the rusty little town
of Dieppe. One dark, unruly night she issued secretly out of a
small postern gate of the castle, which the enemy had neglected
to guard. The postern gate is there to this very day; opening

ville (1595–1663), who was a French general, to join the cause, and also her
two brothers, Louis II. de Bourbon, the Great Condé (1621–86), and Armand
de Bourbon, Prince Conti (1629–66). In 1650, Condé, Conti, and the Duc
de Longueville were arrested, but the Duchess de Longueville escaped and
secured the aid of Turenne (Henri de la Tour d'Auvergne, 1611–75), Marshal
of France, who attempted to release the prisoners. Soon thereafter, all
being weary of the war, Louis XIV. was invited back to Paris, Mazarin was
recalled, and the leaders of the war were obliged to flee.

[1] Twelve thousand men were raised to carry on the war of the Fronde.
By act of Parliament each *porte cochère* ("carriage entrance") was taxed to
furnish one mounted soldier. This cavalry was known as *la cavalerie des
portes cochères;* that is, the cavalry, or chivalry, of the carriage entrances.

[2] A town of France near Paris. The castle of Vincennes, erected in the
midst of a forest, at first used as a royal residence, was later made a state
prison.

[3] A seaport of France on the English Channel, at one time the principal
port of France.

upon a narrow bridge over a deep fosse between the castle and the brow of the hill. She was followed by her female attendants, a few domestics, and some gallant cavaliers, who still remained faithful to her fortunes. Her object was to gain a small port about two leagues distant, where she had privately provided a vessel for her escape in case of emergency.

"The little band of fugitives were obliged to perform the distance on foot. When they arrived at the port the wind was high and stormy, the tide contrary, the vessel anchored far off in the road, and no means of getting on board but by a fishing shallop which lay tossing like a cockle shell on the edge of the surf. The Duchess determined to risk the attempt. The seamen endeavored to dissuade her, but the imminence of her danger on shore, and the magnanimity of her spirit, urged her on. She had to be borne to the shallop in the arms of a mariner. Such was the violence of the wind and waves that he faltered, lost his foothold, and let his precious burden fall into the sea.

"The Duchess was nearly drowned, but partly through her own struggles, partly by the exertions of the seamen, she got to land. As soon as she had a little recovered strength, she insisted on renewing the attempt. The storm, however, had by this time become so violent as to set all efforts at defiance. To delay was to be discovered and taken prisoner. As the only resource left, she procured horses, mounted with her female attendants, *en croupe*,[1] behind the gallant gentlemen who accompanied her, and scoured the country to seek some temporary asylum.

"While the Duchess," continued the Marquis, laying his forefinger on my uncle's breast to arouse his flagging attention — "while the Duchess, poor lady, was wandering amid the tempest in this disconsolate manner, she arrived at this chateau. Her approach caused some uneasiness; for the clattering of a troop of horse at dead of night up the avenue of a lonely chateau, in those unsettled times, and in a troubled part of the country, was enough to occasion alarm.

[1] On pillions, or pads, behind the saddle.

"A tall, broad-shouldered chasseur, armed to the teeth, galloped ahead, and announced the name of the visitor. All uneasiness was dispelled. The household turned out with flambeaux to receive her, and never did torches gleam on a more weather-beaten, travel-stained band than came tramping into the court. Such pale, careworn faces, such bedraggled dresses, as the poor Duchess and her females presented, each seated behind her cavalier; while the half drenched, half drowsy pages and attendants seemed ready to fall from their horses with sleep and fatigue.

"The Duchess was received with a hearty welcome by my ancestor. She was ushered into the hall of the chateau, and the fires soon crackled and blazed, to cheer herself and her train; and every spit and stewpan was put in requisition to prepare ample refreshment for the wayfarers.

"She had a right to our hospitalities," continued the Marquis, drawing himself up with a slight degree of stateliness, "for she was related to our family. I'll tell you how it was. Her father, Henry de Bourbon, Prince of Condé "[1]—

"But did the Duchess pass the night in the chateau?" said my uncle rather abruptly, terrified at the idea of getting involved in one of the Marquis's genealogical discussions.

"Oh, as to the Duchess, she was put into the very apartment you occupied last night, which at that time was a kind of state apartment. Her followers were quartered in the chambers opening upon the neighboring corridor, and her favorite page slept in an adjoining closet. Up and down the corridor walked the great chasseur who had announced her arrival, and who acted as a kind of sentinel or guard. He was a dark, stern, powerful-looking fellow; and as the light of a lamp in the corridor fell upon his deeply marked face and sinewy form, he seemed capable of defending the castle with his single arm.

"It was a rough, rude night, about this time of the year—

[1] Henry de Bourbon, Prince of Condé (1552–58), father of the Duchess de Longueville, and of the Grand Condé and the Prince of Conti.

apropos ! now I think of it, last night was the anniversary of her
visit. I may well remember the precise date, for it was a night
not to be forgotten by our house. There is a singular tradition
concerning it in our family."   Here the Marquis hesitated, and
a cloud seemed to gather about his bushy eyebrows.   "There is
a tradition — that a strange occurrence took place that night, — a
strange, mysterious, inexplicable occurrence "— Here he checked
himself, and paused.

"Did it relate to that lady ? " inquired my uncle eagerly.

"It was past the hour of midnight," resumed the Marquis,
"when the whole chateau "— Here he paused again. My uncle
made a movement of anxious curiosity.

"Excuse me," said the Marquis, a slight blush streaking his
sallow visage.   "There are some circumstances connected with
our family history which I do not like to relate.   That was a
rude period, a time of great crimes among great men ; for you
know high blood, when it runs wrong, will not run tamely, like
blood of the *canaille.*[1]   Poor lady ! But I have a little family
pride, that — excuse me — we will change the subject, if you
please."

My uncle's curiosity was piqued. The pompous and magnificent introduction had led him to expect something wonderful in
the story to which it served as a kind of avenue. He had no
idea of being cheated out of it by a sudden fit of unreasonable
squeamishness.   Besides, being a traveler in quest of information, he considered it his duty to inquire into everything.

The Marquis, however, evaded every question.

"Well," said my uncle, a little petulantly, "whatever you may
think of it, I saw that lady last night."

The Marquis stepped back and gazed at him with surprise.

"She paid me a visit in my bedchamber."

The Marquis pulled out his snuffbox with a shrug and a smile,
taking this, no doubt, for an awkward piece of English pleasantry,
which politeness required him to be charmed with.

---

[1] Lowest class of people.

My uncle went on gravely, however, and related the whole circumstance. The Marquis heard him through with profound attention, holding his snuffbox unopened in his hand. When the story was finished, he tapped on the lid of his box deliberately, took a long, sonorous pinch of snuff—

"Bah !" said the Marquis, and walked towards the other end of the gallery.

Here the narrator paused. The company waited for some time for him to resume his narration ; but he continued silent.

"Well," said the inquisitive gentleman, "and what did your uncle say then ? "

"Nothing," replied the other.

"And what did the Marquis say further ? "

"Nothing."

"And is that all ? "

"That is all," said the narrator, filling a glass of wine.

"I surmise," said the shrewd old gentleman with the waggish nose, "I surmise the ghost must have been the old housekeeper, walking her rounds to see that all was right."

"Bah !" said the narrator. "My uncle was too much accustomed to strange sights not to know a ghost from a housekeeper."

There was a murmur round the table, half of merriment, half of disappointment. I was inclined to think the old gentleman had really an after part of his story in reserve ; but he sipped his wine and said nothing more ; and there was an odd expression about his dilapidated countenance which left me in doubt whether he were in drollery or earnest.

"Egad," said the knowing gentleman with the flexible nose, "this story of your uncle puts me in mind of one that used to be told of an aunt of mine, by the mother's side ; though I don't know that it will bear a comparison, as the good lady was not so prone to meet with strange adventures. But at any rate you shall have it."

THE ADVENTURE OF MY AUNT.

MY aunt was a lady of large frame, strong mind, and great resolution. She was what might be termed a very manly woman. My uncle was a thin, puny little man, very meek and acquiescent, and no match for my aunt. It was observed that he dwindled and dwindled gradually away, from the day of his marriage. His wife's powerful mind was too much for him; it wore him out. My aunt, however, took all possible care of him; had half the doctors in town to prescribe for him; made him take all their prescriptions, and dosed him with physic enough to cure a whole hospital. All was in vain. My uncle grew worse and worse the more dosing and nursing he underwent, until in the end he added another to the long list of matrimonial victims who have been killed with kindness.

"And was it his ghost that appeared to her?" asked the inquisitive gentleman, who had questioned the former story-teller.

"You shall hear," replied the narrator.—My aunt took on mightily for the death of her poor dear husband. Perhaps she felt some compunction at having given him so much physic, and nursed him into the grave. At any rate, she did all that a widow could do to honor his memory. She spared no expense in either the quantity or quality of her mourning weeds; wore a miniature of him about her neck as large as a little sundial, and had a full-length portrait of him always hanging in her bedchamber. All the world extolled her conduct to the skies; and it was determined that a woman who behaved so well to the memory of one husband deserved soon to get another.

It was not long after this that she went to take up her residence in an old country seat in Derbyshire,[1] which had long been in the care of merely a steward and housekeeper. She took most of

---

[1] Derbyshire, or Derby, is a county of England, whose capital, Derby, is thirty-five miles northeast of Birmingham.

her servants with her, intending to make it her principal abode. The house stood in a lonely, wild part of the country, among the gray Derbyshire hills, with a murderer hanging in chains on a bleak height in full view.

The servants from town were half frightened out of their wits at the idea of living in such a dismal, pagan-looking place; especially when they got together in the servants' hall in the evening, and compared notes on all the hobgoblin stories picked up in the course of the day. They were afraid to venture alone about the gloomy, black-looking chambers. My lady's maid, who was troubled with nerves, declared she could never sleep alone in such a "gashly,[1] rummaging old building;" and the footman, who was a kind-hearted young fellow, did all in his power to cheer her up. .

My aunt was struck with the lonely appearance of the house. Before going to bed, therefore, she examined well the fastnesses of the doors and windows; locked up the plate with her own hands, and carried the keys, together with a little box of money and jewels, to her own room; for she was a notable woman, and always saw to all things herself. Having put the keys under her pillow, and dismissed her maid, she sat by her toilet arranging her hair; for being, in spite of her grief for my uncle, rather a buxom widow, she was somewhat particular about her person. She sat for a little while looking at her face in the glass, first on one side, then on the other, as ladies are apt to do when they would ascertain whether they have been in good looks; for a roistering country squire of the neighborhood, with whom she had flirted when a girl, had called that day to welcome her to the country.

All of a sudden she thought she heard something move behind her. She looked hastily round, but there was nothing to be seen. Nothing but the grimly painted portrait of her poor dear man, hanging against the wall.

She gave a heavy sigh to his memory, as she was accustomed

[1] Ghastly.

to do whenever she spoke of him in company, and then went on
adjusting her nightdress, and thinking of the squire.   Her sigh
was reëchoed, or answered, by a long-drawn breath.   She looked
round again, but no one was to be seen.   She ascribed these
sounds to the wind oozing through the rat holes of the old mansion, and proceeded leisurely to put her hair in papers, when, all
at once, she thought she perceived one of the eyes of the portrait
move.

"The back of her head being towards it!" said the story-teller
with the ruined head,—"good!"

"Yes, sir," replied dryly the narrator, "her back being towards
the portrait, but her eyes fixed on its reflection in the glass."—
Well, as I was saying, she perceived one of the eyes of the portrait move.   So strange a circumstance, as you may well suppose,
gave her a sudden shock.   To assure herself of the fact, she put
one hand to her forehead as if rubbing it; peeped through her
fingers, and moved the candle with the other hand.   The light
of the taper gleamed on the eye, and was reflected from it.   She
was sure it moved.   Nay, more, it seemed to give her a wink,
as she had sometimes known her husband to do when living!
It struck a momentary chill to her heart; for she was a lone woman, and felt herself fearfully situated.

The chill was but transient.   My aunt, who was almost as resolute a personage as your uncle, sir [turning to the old story-teller],
became instantly calm and collected.   She went on adjusting her
dress.   She even hummed an air, and did not make even a single
false note.   She casually overturned a dressing box; took a candle and picked up the articles one by one from the floor; pursued
a rolling pincushion that was making the best of its way under
the bed; then opened the door; looked for an instant into the
corridor, as if in doubt whether to go; and then walked quietly
out.

She hastened downstairs, ordered the servants to arm themselves with the weapons first at hand, placed herself at their head,
and returned almost immediately.

Her hastily levied army presented a formidable force. The steward had a rusty blunderbuss, the coachman a loaded whip, the footman a pair of horse pistols, the cook a huge chopping knife, and the butler a bottle in each hand. My aunt led the van with a red-hot poker, and in my opinion she was the most formidable of the party. The waiting maid, who dreaded to stay alone in the servants' hall, brought up the rear, smelling to a broken bottle of volatile salts, and expressing her terror of the "ghostesses." "Ghosts!" said my aunt resolutely. "I'll singe their whiskers for them!"

They entered the chamber. All was still and undisturbed as when she had left it. They approached the portrait of my uncle. "Pull down that picture!" cried my aunt. A heavy groan, and a sound like the chattering of teeth, issued from the portrait. The servants shrunk back; the maid uttered a faint shriek, and clung to the footman for support.

"Instantly!" added my aunt, with a stamp of the foot.

The picture was pulled down, and from a recess behind it, in which had formerly stood a clock, they hauled forth a round-shouldered, black-bearded varlet, with a knife as long as my arm, but trembling all over like an aspen leaf.

"Well, and who was he? No ghost, I suppose," said the inquisitive gentleman.

"A knight of the post,"[1] replied the narrator, "who had been smitten with the worth of the wealthy widow; or rather, a marauding Tarquin,[2] who had stolen into her chamber to violate her purse, and rifle her strong box, when all the house should be asleep. In plain terms," continued he, "the vagabond was a loose, idle fellow of the neighborhood, who had once been a servant in the house, and had been employed to assist in arranging

[1] "Knight of the post," i.e., an offender who has been punished at the whipping post; hence, a sharper in general.

[2] Tarquin the Proud, Lucius Tarquinius Superbus, seventh and last king of Rome (died about B.C. 495). His reign was characterized by bloodshed, violence, and aggressive warfare.

it for the reception of its mistress.   He confessed that he had
contrived this hiding place for his nefarious purpose, and had bor-
rowed an eye from the portrait by way of a reconnoitering hole."

"And what did they do with him ?   Did they hang him ? "
resumed the questioner.

"Hang him !   How could they ? " exclaimed a beetle-browed [1]
barrister with a hawk's nose.   "The offense was not capital.
No robbery, no assault had been committed.   No forcible entry
or breaking into the premises " —

"My aunt," said the narrator, "was a woman of spirit, and
apt to take the law in her own hands.   She had her own notions
of cleanliness also.   She ordered the fellow to be drawn through
the horsepond, to cleanse away all offenses, and then to be well
rubbed down with an oaken towel." [2]

"And what became of him afterwards ? " said the inquisitive
gentleman.

"I do not exactly know.   I believe he was sent on a voyage
of improvement to Botany Bay." [3]

"And your aunt ? " said the inquisitive gentleman.   "I'll warrant she took care to make her maid sleep in the room with her
after that."

"No, sir, she did better; she gave her hand shortly after to the
roistering squire; for she used to observe that it was a dismal
thing for a woman to sleep alone in the country."

"She was right," observed the inquisitive gentleman, nodding
sagaciously; "but I am sorry they did not hang that fellow."

It was agreed on all hands that the last narrator had brought
his tale to the most satisfactory conclusion, though a country
clergyman present regretted that the uncle and aunt, who figured
in the different stories, had not been married together; they cer-
tainly would have been well matched.

[1] Having shaggy, overhanging eyebrows, like the antennæ of beetles.
[2] "An oaken towel," i.e., a cudgel.
[3] A harbor on the eastern coast of Australia, where there is an English
convict settlement.

"But I don't see, after all," said the inquisitive gentleman, "that there was any ghost in this last story."

"Oh, if it's ghosts you want, honey," cried the Irish Captain of Dragoons, "if it's ghosts you want, you shall have a whole regiment of them. And since these gentlemen have given the adventures of their uncles and aunts, faith, and I'll even give you a chapter out of my own family history."

THE BOLD DRAGOON;

OR,

THE ADVENTURE OF MY GRANDFATHER.

MY grandfather was a bold dragoon, for it's a profession, d'ye see, that has run in the family. All my forefathers have been dragoons, and died on the field of honor, except myself, and I hope my posterity may be able to say the same; however, I don't mean to be vainglorious. Well, my grandfather, as I said, was a bold dragoon, and had served in the Low Countries.[1] In fact, he was one of that very army which, according to my uncle Toby,[2] swore so terribly in Flanders. He could swear a good stick[3] himself; and, moreover, was the very man that introduced the doctrine Corporal Trim[4] mentions of radical heat and radical moisture, or, in other words, the mode of keeping out the damps of ditch water by burnt brandy. Be that as it may, it's nothing

[1] Another name for the Netherlands.

[2] Uncle Toby, a character in Sterne's Tristram Shandy, was a captain who was wounded at the siege of Namur in Flanders, and was obliged to retire from the service, but who was always indulging in reminiscences about the battle (see Tristram Shandy, vol. iii., chap. xi.).

[3] "A good stick," i.e., a good deal.

[4] Corporal Trim was Uncle Toby's attendant, and was represented as faithful, simple-minded, and affectionate. For his doctrine of radical heat and radical moisture, see Tristram Shandy, vol. v., chap. xxxviii.

to the purport of my story. I only tell it to show you that my grandfather was a man not easily to be humbugged. He had seen service, or, according to his own phrase, he had seen the devil, and that's saying everything.

Well, gentlemen, my grandfather was on his way to England, for which he intended to embark from Ostend [1]—bad luck to the place ! for one where I was kept by storms and head winds for three long days, and the devil of a [2] jolly companion or pretty girl to comfort me. Well, as I was saying, my grandfather was on his way to England, or rather to Ostend—no matter which, it's all the same. So one evening, towards nightfall, he rode jollily into Bruges.[3] Very like you all know Bruges, gentlemen ; a queer, old-fashioned, Flemish [4] town, once, they say, a great place for trade and money-making in old times, when the Mynheers were in their glory; but almost as large and as empty as an Irishman's pocket at the present day. Well, gentlemen, it was at the time of the annual fair. All Bruges was crowded ; and the canals swarmed with Dutch boats, and the streets swarmed with Dutch merchants ; and there was hardly any getting along for goods, wares, and merchandises, and peasants in big breeches, and women in half a score of petticoats.

My grandfather rode jollily along, in his easy, slashing way; for he was a saucy, sunshiny fellow, staring about him at the motley crowd, and the old houses with gable ends to the street, and storks' nests in the chimneys ; winking at the juffrouws [5] who showed their faces at the windows, and joking the women right and left in the street ; all of whom laughed, and took it in amazing good part ; for though he did not know a word of the language, yet he had always a knack of making himself understood among the women.

[1] A seaport town of Belgium in West Flanders.
[2] " The devil of a," a phrase used to contradict a statement.
[3] The capital of the province of West Flanders in Belgium. It owes its name to the number of bridges which cross its canals.
[4] Pertaining to Flanders.   [5] Young ladies.

Well, gentlemen, it being the time of the annual fair, all the town was crowded, every inn and tavern full, and my grandfather applied in vain from one to the other for admittance. At length he rode up to an old rickety inn, that looked ready to fall to pieces, and which all the rats would have run away from if they could have found room in any other house to put their heads. It was just such a queer building as you see in Dutch pictures, with a tall roof that reached up into the clouds, and as many garrets, one over the other, as the seven heavens of Mahomet.[1] Nothing had saved it from tumbling down but a stork's nest on the chimney, which always brings good luck to a house in the Low Countries; and at the very time of my grandfather's arrival, there were two of these long-legged birds of grace standing like ghosts on the chimney top. Faith, but they've kept the house on its legs to this very day, for you may see it any time you pass through Bruges, as it stands there yet, only it is turned into a brewery of strong Flemish beer, — at least it was so when I came that way after the battle of Waterloo.[2]

My grandfather eyed the house curiously as he approached. It might not have altogether struck his fancy, had he not seen in large letters over the door,

"HIER VERKOOPT MAN GOEDEN DRANK."[3]

My grandfather had learned enough of the language to know that the sign promised good liquor. "This is the house for me," said he, stopping short before the door.

The sudden appearance of a dashing dragoon was an event in

[1] Mahomet, or Mohammed (570–632), the founder of Mohammedanism, a widely diffused religion. He believed in seven heavens, placed one above the other, to which, as alleged by his followers, he made a journey one night, accompanied by the angel Gabriel.

[2] The battle fought in 1815 in which the English and Prussians, under the Duke of Wellington, defeated the French, under Napoleon Bonaparte, and rescued Europe from French domination.

[3] Here good drink is sold.

an old inn frequented only by the peaceful sons of traffic. A rich burgher of Antwerp, a stately, ample man in a broad Flemish hat, and who was the great man and great patron of the establishment, sat smoking a clean, long pipe on one side of the door; a fat little distiller of Geneva,[1] from Schiedam,[2] sat smoking on the other; and the bottle-nosed[3] host stood in the door, and the comely hostess, in crimped cap, beside him; and the hostess's daughter, a plump Flanders lass, with long gold pendants in her ears, was at a side window.

"Humph!" said the rich burgher of Antwerp, with a sulky glance at the stranger.

"De duyvel!"[4] said the fat little distiller of Schiedam.

The landlord saw, with the quick glance of a publican, that the new guest was not at all to the taste of the old ones; and, to tell the truth, he did not like my grandfather's saucy eye. He shook his head. "Not a garret in the house but is full."

"Not a garret!" echoed the landlady.

"Not a garret!" echoed the daughter.

The burgher of Antwerp and the little distiller of Schiedam continued to smoke their pipes sullenly, eying the enemy askance from under their broad hats, but said nothing.

My grandfather was not a man to be browbeaten. He threw the reins on his horse's neck, cocked his head on one side, stuck one arm akimbo. "Faith and troth!" said he, "but I'll sleep in this house this very night." As he said this he gave a slap on his thigh, by way of emphasis. The slap went to the landlady's heart.

He followed up the vow by jumping off his horse, and making his way past the staring Mynheers into the public room. Maybe you've been in the barroom of an old Flemish inn. Faith, but a handsome chamber it was as you'd wish to see; with a brick

---

[1] A strongly alcoholic liquor made in Holland; called also "Hollands."
[2] A town of Holland famed for its gin.
[3] Having a nose bottle-shaped, or large at the end.
[4] The devil.

floor, and a great fireplace, with the whole Bible history in glazed tiles ; and then the mantelpiece, pitching itself head foremost out of the wall, with a whole regiment of cracked teapots and earthen jugs paraded on it; not to mention half a dozen great Delft [1] platters, hung about the room by way of pictures, and the little bar in one corner, and the bouncing barmaid inside of it, with a red calico cap, and yellow eardrops.

My grandfather snapped his fingers over his head, as he cast an eye round the room. " Faith, this is the very house I've been looking after," said he.

There was some further show of resistance on the part of the garrison ; but my grandfather was an old soldier, and an Irishman to boot,[2] and not easily repulsed, especially after he had got into the fortress. So he blarneyed the landlord, kissed the landlord's wife, tickled the landlord's daughter, chucked the barmaid under the chin ; and it was agreed on all hands that it would be a thousand pities, and a burning shame into the bargain, to turn such a bold dragoon into the streets. So they laid their heads together — that is to say, my grandfather and the landlady — and it was at length agreed to accommodate him with an old chamber that had been for some time shut up.

"Some say it's haunted," whispered the landlord's daughter ; "but you are a bold dragoon, and I dare say don't fear ghosts."

"The devil a bit ! " said my grandfather, pinching her plump cheek. " But if I should be troubled by ghosts, I've been to the Red Sea in my time, and have a pleasant way of laying [3] them, my darling."

And then he whispered something to the girl which made her laugh, and give him a good-humored box on the ear. In short, there was nobody knew better how to make his way among the petticoats [4] than my grandfather.

In a little while, as was his usual way, he took complete pos-

---

[1] Pottery made at the city of Delft in Holland.
[2] " To boot," i.e., in addition.
[3] Exorcising.   [4] Women.

session of the house, swaggering all over it; into the stable to look after his horse, into the kitchen to look after his supper. He had something to say or do with every one; smoked with the Dutchmen, drank with the Germans, slapped the landlord on the shoulder, romped with his daughter and the barmaid. Never, since the days of Alley Croaker, had such a rattling blade [1] been seen. The landlord stared at him with astonishment; the landlord's daughter hung her head and giggled whenever he came near; and as he swaggered along the corridor, with his sword trailing by his side, the maids looked after him and whispered to one another, " What a proper [2] man!"

At supper, my grandfather took command of the table d'hôte as though he had been at home; helped everybody, not forgetting himself; talked with every one, whether he understood their language or not; and made his way into the intimacy of the rich burgher of Antwerp, who had never been known to be sociable with any one during his life. In fact, he revolutionized the whole establishment, and gave it such a rouse that the very house reeled with it. He outsat every one at table, excepting the little fat distiller of Schiedam, who sat soaking a long time before he broke forth; but when he did, he was a very devil incarnate. He took a violent affection for my grandfather; so they sat drinking and smoking, and telling stories, and singing Dutch and Irish songs, without understanding a word each other said, until the little Hollander was fairly swamped with his own gin and water, and carried off to bed, whooping and hiccoughing, and trolling the burden of a Low Dutch love song.

Well, gentlemen, my grandfather was shown to his quarters up a large staircase composed of loads of hewn timber; and through long rigmarole [3] passages, hung with blackened paintings of fish and fruit and game, and country frolics, and huge kitchens, and portly burgomasters, such as you see about old-fashioned Flemish inns, till at length he arrived at his room.

1 " Rattling blade," i.e., reckless fellow.
2 Handsome.   3 Confusing.

An old times chamber it was, sure enough, and crowded with all kinds of trumpery. It looked like an infirmary for decayed and superannuated furniture, where everything diseased or disabled was sent to nurse or to be forgotten. Or rather it might be taken for a general congress of old legitimate movables, where every kind and country had a representative. No two chairs were alike. Such high backs, and low backs, and leather bottoms, and worsted bottoms, and straw bottoms, and no bottoms ; and cracked marble tables with curiously carved legs, holding balls in their claws, as though they were going to play at ninepins.

My grandfather made a bow to the motley assemblage as he entered, and, having undressed himself, placed his light in the fireplace, asking pardon of the tongs, which seemed to be making love to the shovel in the chimney corner, and whispering soft nonsense in its ear.

The rest of the guests were by this time sound asleep, for your Mynheers are huge sleepers. The housemaids, one by one, crept up yawning to their attics ; and not a female head in the inn was laid on a pillow that night without dreaming of the bold dragoon.

My grandfather, for his part, got into bed, and drew over him one of those great bags of down, under which they smother a man in the Low Countries ; and there he lay, melting between two feather beds, like an anchovy sandwich between two slices of toast and butter. He was a warm-complexioned man, and this smothering played the very deuce with him.[1] So, sure enough, in a little time it seemed as if a legion of imps were twitching at him, and all the blood in his veins was in a fever heat.

He lay still, however, until all the house was quiet, excepting the snoring of the Mynheers from the different chambers, who answered one another in all kinds of tones and cadences, like so many bullfrogs in a swamp. The quieter the house became the more unquiet became my grandfather. He waxed warmer and warmer, until at length the bed became too hot to hold him.

[1] " Played the very," etc., i.e., annoyed him very much.

"Maybe the maid had warmed it too much ? " said the curious gentleman inquiringly.

"I rather think the contrary," replied the Irishman.   "But, be that as it may, it grew too hot for my grandfather."

"Faith, there's no standing this any longer," says he.   So he jumped out of bed, and went strolling about the house.

"What for ? " said the inquisitive gentleman.

"Why, to cool himself, to be sure—or perhaps to find a more comfortable bed—or perhaps— But no matter what he went for; he never mentioned, and there's no use in taking up our time in conjecturing."

Well, my grandfather had been for some time absent from his room, and was returning, perfectly cool, when just as he reached the door he heard a strange noise within.   He paused and listened.   It seemed as if some one were trying to hum a tune in defiance of the asthma.   He recollected the report of the room being haunted; but he was no believer in ghosts, so he pushed the door gently open and peeped in.

Egad, gentlemen, there was a gambol carrying on within enough to have astonished St. Anthony [1] himself.   By the light of the fire he saw a pale, weazen-faced fellow, in a long flannel gown and a tall white nightcap with a tassel to it, who sat by the fire with a bellows under his arm by way of bagpipe, from which he forced the asthmatical music that had bothered my grandfather.   As he played, too, he kept twitching about with a thousand queer contortions, nodding his head, and bobbing about his tasseled nightcap.

My grandfather thought this very odd and mighty presumptuous, and was about to demand what business he had to play his wind instrument in another gentleman's quarters, when a new cause of astonishment met his eye.   From the opposite side of the room, a long-backed, bandy-legged chair, covered with leather, and studded all over in a coxcombical fashion with little brass

[1] St. Anthony (251–356) was the Egyptian founder of monachism, the doctrine of a life of religious seclusion.

nails, got suddenly into motion, thrust out first a claw foot, then a crooked arm, and at length, making a leg, slid gracefully up to an easy-chair of tarnished brocade, with a hole in its bottom, and led it gallantly out in a ghostly minuet about the floor.

The musician now played fiercer and fiercer, and bobbed his head and his nightcap about like mad. By degrees the dancing mania seemed to seize upon all the other pieces of furniture. The antique, long-bodied chairs paired off in couples and led down a country dance; a three-legged stool danced a hornpipe, though horribly puzzled by its supernumerary limb; while the amorous tongs seized the shovel round the waist, and whirled it about the room in a German waltz. In short, all the movables got in motion, pirouetting hands across, right and left, like so many devils; all except a great clothespress, which kept courtesying and courtesying in a corner, like a dowager, in exquisite time to the music, being rather too corpulent to dance, or perhaps at a loss for a partner.

My grandfather concluded the latter to be the reason; so being, like a true Irishman, devoted to the sex, and at all times ready for a frolic, he bounced into the room, called to the musician to strike up Paddy O'Rafferty,[1] capered up to the clothespress, and seized upon the two handles to lead her out; when—whirr ! the whole revel was at an end. The chairs, tables, tongs, and shovel slunk in an instant as quietly into their places as if nothing had happened, and the musician vanished up the chimney, leaving the bellows behind him in his hurry. My grandfather found himself seated in the middle of the floor, with the clothespress sprawling before him, and the two handles jerked off, and in his hands.

"Then, after all, this was a mere dream," said the inquisitive gentleman.

"The divil a bit of a dream !" replied the Irishman. "There never was a truer fact in this world. Faith, I should have liked to see any man tell my grandfather it was a dream."

Well, gentlemen, as the clothespress was a mighty heavy body,

---

[1] An old popular Irish tune.

and my grandfather likewise, particularly in rear, you may easily suppose that two such heavy bodies coming to the ground would make a bit of a noise. Faith, the old mansion shook as though it had mistaken it for an earthquake. The whole garrison was alarmed. The landlord, who slept below, hurried up with a candle to inquire the cause, but with all his haste his daughter had arrived at the scene of uproar before him. The landlord was followed by the landlady, who was followed by the bouncing barmaid, who was followed by the simpering chambermaids, all holding together, as well as they could, such garments as they first laid hands on; but all in a terrible hurry to see what the deuce was to pay in the chamber of the bold dragoon.

My grandfather related the marvelous scene he had witnessed, and the broken handles of the prostrate clothespress bore testimony to the fact. There was no contesting such evidence; particularly with a lad of my grandfather's complexion, who seemed able to make good every word either with sword or shillalah.[1] So the landlord scratched his head and looked silly, as he was apt to do when puzzled. The landlady scratched — no, she did not scratch her head, but she knit her brow, and did not seem half pleased with the explanation. But the landlady's daughter corroborated it by recollecting that the last person who had dwelt in that chamber was a famous juggler, who died of St. Vitus's dance,[2] and had no doubt infected all the furniture.

This set all things to rights, particularly when the chambermaids declared that they had all witnessed strange carryings on in that room; and as they declared this upon their honors, there could not remain a doubt upon this subject.

"And did your grandfather go to bed again in that room?" said the inquisitive gentleman.

---

[1] A cudgel, so called from Shillelagh, a place in Ireland famous for its oaks.

[2] St. Vitus's dance, or chorea, is a nervous disease marked by involuntary motions. It is called after St. Vitus, a Sicilian child martyr of the early part of the fourth century, who was believed to grant to his devotees relief from the dancing mania, which prevailed during the middle ages.

"'That's more than I can tell. Where he passed the rest of the night was a secret he never disclosed. In fact, though he had seen much service, he was but indifferently acquainted with geography, and apt to make blunders in his travels about inns at night, which it would have puzzled him sadly to account for in the morning."

"Was he ever apt to walk in his sleep ? " said the knowing old gentleman.

"Never that I heard of."

There was a little pause after this rigmarole Irish romance, when the old gentleman with the haunted head observed that the stories hitherto related had rather a burlesque tendency. "I recollect an adventure, however," added he, "which I heard of during a residence at Paris, for the truth of which I can undertake to vouch, and which is of a very grave and singular nature."

ADVENTURE OF THE GERMAN STUDENT.

ON a stormy night, in the tempestuous times of the French Revolution, a young German was returning to his lodgings, at a late hour, across the old part of Paris. The lightning gleamed, and the loud claps of thunder rattled through the lofty narrow streets—but I should first tell you something about this young German.

Gottfried Wolfgang was a young man of good family. He had studied for some time at Göttingen,[1] but being of a visionary and enthusiastic character, he had wandered into those wild and speculative doctrines which have so often bewildered German students. His secluded life, his intense application, and the singular nature of his studies, had an effect on both mind and body. His health was impaired, his imagination diseased.

---

[1] A town of Hanover in Prussia. Its university, founded in 1734, was at one time the chief seat of learning in Germany.

He had been indulging in fanciful speculations on spiritual essences, until, like Swedenborg,[1] he had an ideal world of his own around him. He took up a notion, I do not know from what cause, that there was an evil influence hanging over him; an evil genius or spirit seeking to insnare him and insure his perdition. Such an idea working on his melancholy temperament produced the most gloomy effects. He became haggard and desponding. His friends discovered the mental malady preying upon him, and determined that the best cure was a change of scene; he was sent, therefore, to finish his studies amidst the splendors and gayeties of Paris.

Wolfgang arrived at Paris at the breaking out of the revolution. The popular delirium at first caught his enthusiastic mind, and he was captivated by the political and philosophical theories of the day; but the scenes of blood which followed shocked his sensitive nature, disgusted him with society and the world, and made him more than ever a recluse. He shut himself up in a solitary apartment in the *Pays Latin*,[2] the quarter of students. There, in a gloomy street not far from the monastic walls of the Sorbonne,[3] he pursued his favorite speculations. Sometimes he spent hours together in the great libraries of Paris, those catacombs of departed authors, rummaging among their hoards of dusty and obsolete works in quest of food for his unhealthy appetite. He was, in a manner, a literary ghoul, feeding in the charnel house of decayed literature.

Wolfgang, though solitary and recluse, was of an ardent temperament, but for a time it operated merely upon his imagina-

[1] Emanuel Swedenborg (1688–1772), founder of the New Jerusalem Church. In his later life he lived entirely in a spiritual world, claiming to have direct intercourse with God, whose prophet he believed himself to be.

[2] Latin Quarter; the name of a district of Paris at one time occupied almost exclusively by students.

[3] The Sorbonne, founded by Robert de Sorbon, confessor of Louis XI., was originally a theological college. The building is now occupied by the University of Paris.

tion. He was too shy and ignorant of the world to make any advances to the fair, but he was a passionate admirer of female beauty, and in his lonely chamber would often lose himself in reveries on forms and faces which he had seen, and his fancy would deck out images of loveliness far surpassing the reality.

While his mind was in this excited and sublimated state, a dream produced an extraordinary effect upon him. It was of a female face of transcendent beauty. So strong was the impression made that he dreamed of it again and again. It haunted his thoughts by day, his slumbers by night; in fine, he became passionately enamored of this shadow of a dream. This lasted so long that it became one of those fixed ideas which haunt the minds of melancholy men, and are at times mistaken for madness.

Such was Gottfried Wolfgang, and such his situation at the time I mentioned. He was returning home late one stormy night, through some of the old and gloomy streets of the *Marais*,[1] the ancient part of Paris. The loud claps of thunder rattled among the high houses of the narrow streets. He came to the Place de Grève,[2] the square where public executions are performed. The lightning quivered about the pinnacles of the ancient Hôtel de Ville,[3] and shed flickering gleams over the open space in front. As Wolfgang was crossing the square, he shrank back with horror at finding himself close by the guillotine. It was the height of the reign of terror, when this dreadful instrument of death stood ever ready, and its scaffold was continually running with the blood of the virtuous and the brave.

---

[1] The Marais Quarter was a gloomy, old-fashioned square of Paris, part of what is now known as the Place de Vosges.

[2] Place de Grève, now known as the Place de l'Hôtel de Ville, has always been associated with dark cruelties. The stake, scaffold, and guillotine reigned there at various times.

[3] The Hôtel de Ville, a marvel of architectural beauty, was completed in 1628, and was the great townhall of Paris until destroyed by fire in 1871. It was the usual rallying place of the democratic party during the French revolutions.

It had that very day been actively employed in the work of car-
nage, and there it stood in grim array, amidst a silent and sleeping city, waiting for fresh victims.

Wolfgang's heart sickened within him, and he was turning
shuddering from the horrible engine, when he beheld a shadowy
form, cowering as it were at the foot of the steps which led up
to the scaffold. A succession of vivid flashes of lightning re-
vealed it more distinctly. It was a female figure, dressed in
black. She was seated on one of the lower steps of the scaffold,
leaning forward, her face hid in her lap ; and her long disheveled
tresses, hanging to the ground, streaming with the rain, which fell
in torrents. Wolfgang paused. There was something awful in
this solitary monument of woe. The female had the appearance
of being above the common order. He knew the times to be
full of vicissitude, and that many a fair head, which had once
been pillowed on down, now wandered houseless. Perhaps this
was some poor mourner whom the dreadful ax had rendered
desolate, and who sat here heartbroken on the strand of existence, from which all that was dear to her had been launched
into eternity.

He approached, and addressed her in the accents of sympathy.
She raised her head and gazed wildly at him. What was his
astonishment at beholding, by the bright glare of the lightning,
the very face which had haunted him in his dreams. It was
pale and disconsolate, but ravishingly beautiful.

Trembling with violent and conflicting emotions, Wolfgang
again accosted her. He spoke something of her being exposed
at such an hour of the night, and to the fury of such a storm,
and offered to conduct her to her friends. She pointed to the
guillotine with a gesture of dreadful signification.

" I have no friend on earth ! " said she.

" But you have a home," said Wolfgang.

" Yes—in the grave ! "

The heart of the student melted at the words.

" If a stranger dare make an offer," said he, " without danger of being misunderstood, I would offer my humble dwelling as a shelter; myself as a devoted friend. I am friendless myself in Paris, and a stranger in the land; but if my life could be of service, it is at your disposal, and should be sacrificed before harm or indignity should come to you."

There was an honest earnestness in the young man's manner that had its effect. His foreign accent, too, was in his favor; it showed him not to be a hackneyed inhabitant of Paris. Indeed, there is an eloquence in true enthusiasm that is not to be doubted. The homeless stranger confided herself implicitly to the protection of the student.

He supported her faltering steps across the Pont Neuf,[1] and by the place where the statue of Henry IV. had been overthrown by the populace. The storm had abated, and the thunder rumbled at a distance. All Paris was quiet; that great volcano of human passion slumbered for a while, to gather fresh strength for the next day's eruption. The student conducted his charge through the ancient streets of the *Pays Latin*, and by the dusky walls of the Sorbonne, to the great dingy hotel which he inhabited. The old portress who admitted them stared with surprise at the unusual sight of the melancholy Wolfgang with a female companion.

On entering his apartment, the student, for the first time, blushed at the scantiness and indifference of his dwelling. He had but one chamber, an old-fashioned salon, heavily carved, and fantastically furnished with the remains of former magnificence; for it was one of those hotels in the quarter of the Luxembourg Palace[2] which had once belonged to nobility. It was lumbered with books and papers, and all the usual apparatus of a student, and his bed stood in a recess at one end.

---

[1] A bridge across the Seine. On it stands a statue of Henry IV., erected to replace one which had stood there from 1635 to 1791, when it was knocked down by the populace and converted into pieces of ordnance.

[2] One of the most magnificent palaces in Paris, erected in 1615. During the French Revolution it was converted into a prison for the confinement of noble families.

When lights were brought, and Wolfgang had a better opportunity of contemplating the stranger, he was more than ever intoxicated by her beauty. Her face was pale, but of a dazzling
fairness, set off by a profusion of raven hair that hung clustering about it. Her eyes were large and brilliant, with a singular
expression approaching almost to wildness. As far as her black
dress permitted her shape to be seen, it was of perfect symme-
try. Her whole appearance was highly striking, though she was
dressed in the simplest style. The only thing approaching to
an ornament which she wore was a broad black band round her
neck, clasped by diamonds.

The perplexity now commenced with the student how to dis-
pose of the helpless being thus thrown upon his protection. He
thought of abandoning his chamber to her, and seeking shelter
for himself elsewhere. Still, he was so fascinated by her charms,
there seemed to be such a spell upon his thoughts and senses,
that he could not tear himself from her presence. Her manner,
too, was singular and unaccountable. She spoke no more of the
guillotine. Her grief had abated. The attentions of the student
had first won her confidence, and then, apparently, her heart.
She was evidently an enthusiast like himself, and enthusiasts soon
understand each other.

In the infatuation of the moment Wolfgang avowed his passion for her. He told her the story of his mysterious dream,
and how she had possessed his heart before he had even seen
her. She was strangely affected by his recital, and acknowledged
to have felt an impulse towards him equally unaccountable. It
was the time for wild theory and wild actions. Old prejudices
and superstitions were done away ; everything was under the sway
of the " Goddess of Reason." [1] Among other rubbish of the old
times, the forms and ceremonies of marriage began to be considered superfluous bonds for honorable minds. Social compacts

[1] In the subversion of all existing institutions during the French Revolution, the worship of human reason, personified as the Goddess of Reason,
was instituted as a new religion.

were the vogue. Wolfgang was too much of a theorist not to be tainted by the liberal doctrines of the day.

" Why should we separate ? " said he. " Our hearts are united ; in the eye of reason and honor we are as one. What need is there of sordid forms to bind high souls together ? "

The stranger listened with emotion ; she had evidently received illumination at the same school.

" You have no home nor family," continued he ; " let me be everything to you ; or rather, let us be everything to one another. If form is necessary, form shall be observed, — there is my hand. I pledge myself to you forever."

" Forever ? " said the stranger solemnly.

" Forever ! " repeated Wolfgang.

The stranger clasped the hand extended to her. " Then I am yours," murmured she, and sank upon his bosom.

The next morning the student left his bride sleeping, and sallied forth at an early hour to seek more spacious apartments suitable to the change in his situation. When he returned, he found the stranger lying with her head hanging over the bed, and one arm thrown over it. He spoke to her, but received no reply. He advanced to awaken her from her uneasy posture. On taking her hand it was cold — there was no pulsation — her face was pallid and ghastly. In a word, she was a corpse.

Horrified and frantic, he alarmed the house. A scene of confusion ensued. The police was summoned. As the officer of police entered the room, he started back on beholding the corpse.

" Great heaven ! " cried he, " how did this woman come here ? "

" Do you know anything about her ? " said Wolfgang eagerly.

" Do I ? " exclaimed the officer ; " she was guillotined yesterday."

He stepped forward, undid the black collar round the neck of the corpse, and the head rolled on the floor !

The student burst into a frenzy. " The fiend ! the fiend has gained possession of me ! " shrieked he. " I am lost forever." ·

5

They tried to soothe him, but in vain. He was possessed with the frightful belief that an evil spirit had reanimated the dead body to insnare him. He went distracted, and died in a madhouse.

Here the old gentleman with the haunted head finished his narrative.

" And is this really a fact ? " said the inquisitive gentleman.

" A fact not to be doubted," replied the other. " I had it from the best authority. The student told it me himself. I saw him in a madhouse in Paris."

ADVENTURE OF THE MYSTERIOUS PICTURE.

AS one story of the kind produces another, and as all the company seemed fully engrossed with the subject, and disposed to bring their relatives and ancestors upon the scene, there is no knowing how many more strange adventures we might have heard, had not a corpulent old fox hunter, who had slept soundly through the whole, now suddenly awakened, with a loud and long-drawn yawn. The sound broke the charm ; the ghosts took to flight, as though it had been cockcrowing,[1] and there was a universal move for bed.

" And now for the haunted chamber," said the Irish captain, taking his candle.

" Ay, who's to be the hero of the night ? " said the gentleman with the ruined head.

" That we shall see in the morning," said the old gentleman with the nose. " Whoever looks pale and grizzly will have seen the ghost."

" Well, gentlemen," said the Baronet, " there's many a true thing said in jest ; in fact, one of you will sleep in the room to-night."

" What ! — a haunted room ? — a haunted room ? I claim the

---

[1] The time at which cocks begin to crow ; i.e., the dawn of day, when ghosts were always supposed to disappear.

adventure — and I — and I — and I," said a dozen guests, talking and laughing at the same time.

" No, no," said mine host, " there is a secret about one of my rooms on which I feel disposed to try an experiment; so, gentlemen, none of you shall know who has the haunted chamber until circumstances reveal it. I will not even know it myself, but will leave it to chance and the allotment of the housekeeper. At the same time, if it will be any satisfaction to you, I will observe, for the honor of my paternal mansion, that there's scarcely a chamber in it but is well worthy of being haunted."

We now separated for the night, and each went to his allotted room. Mine was in one wing of the building, and I could not but smile at its resemblance in style to those eventful apartments described in the tales of the supper table. It was spacious and gloomy, decorated with lampblack portraits, a bed of ancient damask, with a tester [1] sufficiently lofty to grace a couch of state, and a number of massive pieces of old-fashioned furniture. I drew a great claw-footed armchair before the wide fireplace; stirred up the fire; sat looking into it, and musing upon the odd stories I had heard, until, partly overcome by the fatigue of the day's hunting, and partly by the wine and wassail of mine host, I fell asleep in my chair.

The uneasiness of my position made my slumber troubled, and laid me at the mercy of all kinds of wild and fearful dreams. Now it was that my perfidious dinner and supper rose in rebellion against my peace. I was hag-ridden [2] by a fat saddle of mutton; a plum pudding weighed like lead upon my conscience; the merry thought of a capon filled me with horrible suggestions; and a deviled leg of a turkey stalked in all kinds of diabolical shapes through my imagination. In short, I had a violent fit of the nightmare. Some strange, indefinite evil seemed hanging over me, which I could not avert; something terrible and loathsome oppressed, me which I could not shake off. I was conscious of being

---

[1] Canopy over a bed.

[2] Ridden by a hag or witch; hence, afflicted with nightmare.

asleep, and strove to rouse myself, but every effort redoubled the evil; until gasping, struggling, almost strangling, I suddenly sprang bolt upright in my chair, and awoke.

The light on the mantelpiece had burned low, and the wick was divided; there was a great winding sheet made by the dripping wax on the side towards me. The disordered taper emitted a broad, flaring flame, and threw a strong light on a painting over the fireplace which I had not hitherto observed. It consisted merely of a head, or rather a face, staring full upon me, with an expression that was startling. It was without a frame, and at the first glance I could hardly persuade myself that it was not a real face thrusting itself out of the dark oaken panel. I sat in my chair gazing at it, and the more I gazed the more it disquieted me. I had never before been affected in the same way by any painting. The emotions it caused were strange and indefinite. They were something like what I have heard ascribed to the eyes of the basilisk, or like that mysterious influence in reptiles termed fascination. I passed my hand over my eyes several times, as if seeking instinctively to brush away the illusion,—in vain. They instantly reverted to the picture, and its chilling, creeping influence over my flesh and blood was redoubled. I looked round the room on other pictures, either to divert my attention, or to see whether the same effect would be produced by them. Some of them were grim enough to produce the effect, if the mere grimness of the painting produced it. No such thing; my eye passed over them all with perfect indifference, but the moment it reverted to this visage over the fireplace, it was as if an electric shock darted through me. The other pictures were dim and faded, but this one protruded from a plain background in the strongest relief, and with wonderful truth of coloring. The expression was that of agony,—the agony of intense bodily pain; but a menace scowled upon the brow, and a few sprinklings of blood added to its ghastliness. Yet it was not all these characteristics; it was some horror of the mind, some inscrutable antipathy awakened by this picture, which harrowed up my feelings.

I tried to persuade myself that this was chimerical; that my brain was confused by the fumes of mine host's good cheer, and in some measure by the odd stories about paintings which had been told at supper.   I determined to shake off these vapors of the mind; rose from my chair; walked about the room; snapped my fingers; rallied myself; laughed aloud.   It was a forced laugh, and the echo of it in the old chamber jarred upon my ear.   I walked to the window, and tried to discern the landscape through the glass.   It was pitch darkness, and a howling storm without, and as I heard the wind moan among the trees, I caught a reflection of this accursed visage in the pane of glass, as though it were staring through the window at me.   Even the reflection of it was thrilling.

How was this vile nervous fit — for such I now persuaded myself it was — to be conquered?   I determined to force myself not to look at the painting, but to undress quickly and get into bed. I began to undress, but in spite of every effort, I could not keep myself from stealing a glance every now and then at the picture; and a glance was sufficient to distress me.   Even when my back was turned to it, the idea of this strange face behind me, peeping over my shoulder, was insupportable.   I threw off my clothes and hurried into bed, but still this visage gazed upon me.   I had a full view of it in my bed, and for some time could not take my eyes from it.   I had grown nervous to a dismal degree.   I put out the light, and tried to force myself to sleep — all in vain. The fire, gleaming up a little, threw an uncertain light about the room, leaving, however, the region of the picture in deep shadow. What, thought I, if this be the chamber about which mine host spoke, as having a mystery reigning over it?   I had taken his words merely as spoken in jest; might they have a real import ? I looked around.   The faintly lighted apartment had all the qualifications requisite for a haunted chamber.   It began in my infected imagination to assume strange appearances; the old portraits turned paler and paler, and blacker and blacker; the streaks of light and shadow thrown among the quaint articles of furniture gave them more singular shapes and characters. There was a huge, dark clothespress of antique form, gorgeous in brass and lustrous with wax, that began to grow oppressive to me.

"Am I, then," thought I, "indeed the hero of the haunted room? Is there really a spell laid upon me, or is this all some contrivance of mine host to raise a laugh at my expense?" The idea of being hag-ridden by my own fancy all night, and then bantered on my haggard looks the next day, was intolerable; but the very idea was sufficient to produce the effect, and to render me still more nervous. "Pish!" said I, "it can be no such thing. How could my worthy host imagine that I, or any man, would be so worried by a mere picture? It is my own diseased imagination that torments me."

I turned in bed, and shifted from side to side, to try to fall asleep; but all in vain. When one cannot get asleep by lying quiet, it is seldom that tossing about will effect the purpose. The fire gradually went out, and left the room in total darkness. Still I had the idea of that inexplicable countenance gazing and keeping watch upon me through the gloom; nay, what was worse, the very darkness seemed to magnify its terrors. It was like having an unseen enemy hanging about one in the night. Instead of having one picture now to worry me, I had a hundred. I fancied it in every direction. "There it is," thought I, "and there! and there! with its horrible and mysterious expression still gazing and gazing on me! No; if I must suffer the strange and dismal influence, it were better face a single foe than thus be haunted by a thousand images of it."

Whoever has been in a state of nervous agitation must know that the longer it continues the more uncontrollable it grows. The very air of the chamber seemed at length infected by the baleful presence of this picture. I fancied it hovering over me. I almost felt the fearful visage from the wall approaching my face; it seemed breathing upon me. "This is not to be borne," said I at length, springing out of bed. "I can stand this no longer; I shall only tumble and toss about here all night, make a very specter of myself, and become the hero of the haunted chamber in good earnest. Whatever be the ill consequences, I'll quit this cursed room and seek a night's rest elsewhere. They can but laugh at me, at all events, and they'll be sure to have the laugh upon me if I pass a sleepless night, and show them a haggard and woe-begone visage in the morning."

All this was half muttered to myself as I hastily slipped on my clothes, which having done, I groped my way out of the room and downstairs to the drawing-room. Here, after tumbling over two or three pieces of furniture, I made out to reach a sofa, and stretching myself upon it, determined to bivouac there for the night. The moment I found myself out of the neighborhood of that strange picture, it seemed as if the charm were broken. All its influence was at an end. I felt assured that it was confined to its own dreary chamber, for I had, with a sort of instinctive caution, turned the key when I closed the door. I soon calmed down, therefore, into a state of tranquillity; from that into a drowsiness; and finally into a deep sleep, out of which I did not awake until the housemaid, with her besom [1] and her matin song, came to put the room in order. She stared at finding me stretched upon the sofa, but I presume circumstances of the kind were not uncommon after hunting dinners in her master's bachelor establishment, for she went on with her song and her work, and took no further heed of me.

I had an unconquerable repugnance to return to my chamber; so I found my way to the butler's quarters, made my toilet in the best way circumstances would permit, and was among the first to appear at the breakfast table. Our breakfast was a substantial fox hunter's repast, and the company generally assembled at it. When ample justice had been done to the tea, coffee, cold meats, and humming ale — for all these were furnished in abundance, according to the tastes of the different guests — the conversation began to break out with all the liveliness and freshness of morning mirth.

[1] Broom.

" But who is the hero of the haunted chamber ? who has seen the ghost last night ? " said the inquisitive gentleman, rolling his lobster eyes about the table.

The question set every tongue in motion ; a vast deal of bantering, criticising of countenances, of mutual accusation and retort, took place. Some had drunk deep, and some were unshaven, so that there were suspicious faces enough in the assembly. I alone could not enter with ease and vivacity into the joke ; I felt tongue-tied, embarrassed. A recollection of what I had seen and felt the preceding night still haunted my mind. It seemed as if the mysterious picture still held a thrall upon me. I thought also that our host's eye was turned on me with an air of curiosity. In short, I was conscious that I was the hero of the night, and felt as if every one might read it in my looks. The joke, however, passed over, and no suspicion seemed to attach to me. I was just congratulating myself on my escape, when a servant came in, saying that the gentleman who had slept on the sofa in the drawing-room had left his watch under one of the pillows. My repeater was in his hand.

" What ! " said the inquisitive gentleman, " did any gentleman sleep on the sofa ? "

" Soho, soho ! a hare, a hare ! " [1] cried the old gentleman with the flexible nose.

I could not avoid acknowledging the watch, and was rising in great confusion, when a boisterous old squire who sat beside me exclaimed, slapping me on the shoulder, " 'Sblood, lad, thou art the man as has seen the ghost ! "

The attention of the company was immediately turned on me. If my face had been pale the moment before, it now glowed almost to burning. I tried to laugh, but could only make a grimace, and found the muscles of my face twitching at sixes and sevens,[2] and totally out of all control.

It takes but little to raise a laugh among a set of fox hunters.

[1] A sportsman's cry on the discovery of a hare.
[2] "At sixes and sevens," i.e., in confusion.

There was a world of merriment and joking on the subject, and as I never relished a joke overmuch when it was at my own expense, I began to feel a little nettled. I tried to look cool and calm, and to restrain my pique; but the coolness and calmness of a man in a passion are confounded[1] treacherous.

"Gentlemen," said I, with a slight cocking of the chin and a bad attempt at a smile, "this is all very pleasant — ha, ha ! — very pleasant; but I'd have you know, I am as little superstitious as any of you—ha, ha !—and as to anything like timidity— you may smile, gentlemen, but I trust there's no one here means to insinuate that—as to a room's being haunted—I repeat, gentlemen [growing a little warm at seeing a cursed grin breaking out round me], as to a room's being haunted, I have as little faith in such silly stories as any one. But, since you put the matter home to me, I will say that I have met with something in my room strange and inexplicable to me. [A shout of laughter.] Gentlemen, I am serious; I know well what I am saying; I am calm, gentlemen [striking my fist upon the table], by Heaven, I am calm ! I am neither trifling, nor do I wish to be trifled with. [The laughter of the company suppressed, and with ludicrous attempts at gravity.] There is a picture in the room in which I was put last night that has had an effect upon me the most singular and incomprehensible."

"A picture ? " said the old gentleman with the haunted head. "A picture !" cried the narrator with the nose. "A picture ! a picture !" echoed several voices. Here there was an ungovernable peal of laughter. I could not contain myself. I started up from my seat, looked round on the company with fiery indignation, thrust both of my hands into my pockets, and strode up to one of the windows as though I would have walked through it. I stopped short, looked out upon the landscape without distinguishing a feature of it, and felt my gorge[2] rising almost to suffocation.

Mine host saw it was time to interfere. He had maintained an

---

[1] Confoundedly; extremely.   [2] Indignation.

air of gravity through the whole of the scene; and now stepped forth, as if to shelter me from the overwhelming merriment of my companions.

"Gentlemen," said he, "I dislike to spoil sport, but you have had your laugh, and the joke of the haunted chamber has been enjoyed. I must now take the part of my guest. I must not only vindicate him from your pleasantries, but I must reconcile him to himself, for I suspect he is a little out of humor with his own feelings; and, above all, I must crave his pardon for having made him the subject of a kind of experiment. Yes, gentlemen, there is something strange and peculiar in the chamber to which our friend was shown last night; there is a picture in my house which possesses a singular and mysterious influence, and with which there is connected a very curious story. It is a picture to which I attach a value from a variety of circumstances; and though I have often been tempted to destroy it, from the odd and uncomfortable sensations which it produces in every one that beholds it, yet I have never been able to prevail upon myself to make the sacrifice. It is a picture I never like to look upon myself, and which is held in awe by all my servants. I have therefore banished it to a room but rarely used, and should have had it covered last night, had not the nature of our conversation, and the whimsical talk about a haunted chamber, tempted me to let it remain, by way of experiment, to see whether a stranger, totally unacquainted with its story, would be affected by it."

The words of the Baronet had turned every thought into a different channel. All were anxious to hear the story of the mysterious picture; and, for myself, so strangely were my feelings interested, that I forgot to feel piqued at the experiment my host had made upon my nerves, and joined eagerly in the general entreaty. As the morning was stormy, and denied all egress, my host was glad of any means of entertaining his company; so, drawing his armchair towards the fire, he began.

ADVENTURE OF THE MYSTERIOUS STRANGER.

MANY years since, when I was a young man, and had just left Oxford, I was sent on the grand tour to finish my education. I believe my parents had tried in vain to inoculate me with wisdom; so they sent me to mingle with society, in hopes that I might take it the natural way. Such, at least, appears the reason for which nine tenths of our youngsters are sent abroad.

In the course of my tour I remained some time at Venice. The romantic character of that place delighted me; I was very much amused by the air of adventure and intrigue prevalent in this region of masks and gondolas; and I was exceedingly smitten by a pair of languishing black eyes, that played upon my heart from under an Italian mantle; so I persuaded myself that I was lingering at Venice to study men and manners; at least I persuaded my friends so, and that answered all my purposes.

I was a little prone to be struck by peculiarities in character and conduct, and my imagination was so full of romantic associations with Italy that I was always on the lookout for adventure. Everything chimed in with such a humor in this old mermaid of a city. My suite of apartments were in a proud, melancholy palace on the Grand Canal, formerly the residence of a magnifico,[1] and sumptuous with the traces of decayed grandeur. My gondolier was one of the shrewdest of his class, active, merry, intelligent, and, like his brethren, secret as the grave; that is to say, secret to all the world except his master. I had not had him a week before he put me behind all the curtains in Venice.[2] I liked the silence and mystery of the place, and when I

---

[1] A nobleman or grandee of Venice, so called in courtesy.

[2] " Put me behind," etc., i.e., told me all the secrets and private affairs of the people of Venice.

sometimes saw from my window a black gondola gliding mysteriously along in the dusk of the evening, with nothing visible but its little glimmering lantern, I would jump into my own zendeletta,[1] and give a signal for pursuit. "But I am running away from my subject with the recollection of youthful follies," said the Baronet, checking himself. "Let us come to the point."

Among my familiar resorts was a cassino under the arcades on one side of the grand Square of St. Mark.[2] Here I used frequently to lounge and take my ice, on those warm summer nights when, in Italy, everybody lives abroad until morning. I was seated here one evening when a group of Italians took their seats at a table on the opposite side of the saloon. Their conversation was gay and animated, and carried on with Italian vivacity and gesticulation. I remarked among them one young man, however, who appeared to take no share and find no enjoyment in the conversation, though he seemed to force himself to attend to it. He was tall and slender, and of extremely prepossessing appearance. His features were fine, though emaciated. He had a profusion of black glossy hair, that curled lightly about his head, and contrasted with the extreme paleness of his countenance. His brow was haggard; deep furrows seemed to have been plowed into his visage by care, not by age, for he was evidently in the prime of youth. His eye was full of expression and fire, but wild and unsteady. He seemed to be tormented by some strange fancy or apprehension. In spite of every effort to fix his attention on the conversation of his companions, I noticed that every now and then he would turn his head slowly round, give a glance over his shoulder, and then withdraw it with a sudden jerk, as if something painful met his eye. This was repeated at intervals of about a minute, and he appeared hardly

---

[1] Small boat.

[2] The Square of St. Mark, or Piazza di San Marco, the principal promenade of Venice, is nearly surrounded by the sea. Magnificent churches and palaces occupy the square, and around it extends a vast gallery containing many elegant shops and cafés.

to have recovered from one shock before I saw him slowly preparing to encounter another.

After sitting some time in the cassino, the party paid for the refreshment they had taken, and departed. The young man was the last to leave the saloon, and I remarked him glancing behind him in the same way, just as he passed out of the door. I could not resist the impulse to rise and follow him; for I was at an age when a romantic feeling of curiosity is easily awakened. The party walked slowly down the arcades, talking and laughing as they went. They crossed the Piazzetta,[1] but paused in the middle of it to enjoy the scene. It was one of those moonlight nights, so brilliant and clear in the pure atmosphere of Italy. The moonbeams streamed on the tall tower [2] of St. Mark, and lighted up the magnificent front and swelling domes of the cathedral.[3] The party expressed their delight in animated terms. I kept my eye upon the young man. He alone seemed abstracted and self-occupied. I noticed the same singular and, as it were, furtive, glance over the shoulder which had attracted my attention in the cassino. The party moved on, and I followed. They passed along the walk called the Broglio, turned the corner of the Ducal Palace,[4] and getting into the gondola, glided swiftly away.

The countenance and conduct of this young man dwelt upon my mind, and interested me exceedingly. I met him a day or two afterwards in a gallery of paintings. He was evidently a connoisseur, for he always singled out the most masterly productions, and a few remarks drawn from him by his companions showed an intimate acquaintance with the art. His own taste,

[1] The Piazzetta (" small square ") runs at right angles from the southeast corner of the Piazza of St. Mark to the Grand Canal.

[2] The famous clock tower of the Square of St. Mark, which has on its face a dial resplendent with gold. It was built in 1494 and restored in 1859.

[3] The St. Mark Cathedral, one of the most magnificent in the world.

[4] The Ducal Palace, or Palace of the Doges, is a magnificent structure, first built in 800. It has been destroyed five times, and each time restored with greater splendor. The Broglio is the lower gallery, or piazza, under the Ducal Palace.

however, ran on singular extremes; on Salvator Rosa,[1] in his most savage and solitary scenes; on Raphael,[1] Titian,[1] and Correggio,[1] in their softest delineations of female beauty; on these he would occasionally gaze with transient enthusiasm. But this seemed only a momentary forgetfulness. Still would recur that cautious glance behind, and always quickly withdrawn, as though something terrible met his view.

I encountered him frequently afterwards at the theater, at balls, at concerts; at promenades in the gardens of San Georgio;[2] at the grotesque exhibitions in the Square of St. Mark; among the throng of merchants on the exchange by the Rialto.[3] He seemed, in fact, to seek crowds; to hunt after bustle and amusement; yet never to take any interest in either the business or the gayety of the scene. Ever an air of painful thought, of wretched abstraction; and ever that strange and recurring movement of glancing fearfully over the shoulder. I did not know at first but this might be caused by apprehension of arrest; or, perhaps, from dread of assassination. But if so, why should he go thus continually abroad? Why expose himself at all times and in all places?

I became anxious to know this stranger. I was drawn to him by that romantic sympathy which sometimes draws young men towards each other. His melancholy threw a charm about him, no doubt heightened by the touching expression of his counte-

---

[1] Salvator Rosa was a renowned Italian painter (1615-73) of the Neapolitan school. He had a special skill in depicting strange, wild, turbulent scenes. Sanzio Raphael (1483-1520), an eminent Italian painter, spent much time in decorating churches and altars, and is especially famed for his pictures of the Madonna and the Holy Family. Titian, or Tiziano Vecellio (1477-1576), a celebrated Venetian painter, called " the divine one," excelled chiefly in the depth and beauty of his coloring. Antonio Allegri da Correggio (1494-1534), a great Italian painter, painted many types of female loveliness.

[2] One of the islands in the southern part of Venice, on which is situated the beautiful church of San Georgio Maggiore.

[3] An island on one side of the Grand Canal of Venice. It is the site on which Venice as a city first existed. It is a central point of trade and commerce.

nance, and the manly graces of his person ; for manly beauty has its effect even upon men.   I had an Englishman's habitual diffidence and awkwardness to contend with ; but from frequently meeting him in the cassinos, I gradually edged myself into his acquaintance.   I had no reserve on his part to contend with. He seemed, on the contrary, to court society ; and, in fact, to seek anything rather than be alone.

When he found that I really took an interest in him, he threw himself entirely on my friendship.   He clung to me like a drowning man.   He would walk with me for hours up and down the Place of St. Mark ; or would sit, until night was far advanced, in my apartments.   He took rooms under the same roof with me ; and his constant request was that I would permit him, when it did not incommode me, to sit by me in my saloon.   It was not that he seemed to take a particular delight in my conversation, but rather that he craved the vicinity of a human being, and, above all, of a being that sympathized with him.   " I have often heard," said he, " of the sincerity of Englishmen ; thank God I have one at length for a friend ! "

Yet he never seemed disposed to avail himself of my sympathy other than by mere companionship.   He never sought to unbosom himself to me.   There appeared to be a settled, corroding anguish in his bosom that neither could be soothed "by silence nor by speaking."

A devouring melancholy preyed upon his heart, and seemed to be drying up the very blood in his veins.   It was not a soft melancholy, the disease of the affections, but a parching, withering agony.   I could see at times that his mouth was dry and feverish ; he panted rather than breathed ; his eyes were bloodshot ; his cheeks pale and livid, with now and then faint streaks of red athwart them, — baleful gleams of the fire that was consuming his heart.   As my arm was within his, I felt him press it at times with a convulsive motion to his side ; his hands would clinch themselves involuntarily, and a kind of shudder would run through his frame.

I reasoned with him about his melancholy; sought to draw
from him the cause; he shrunk from all confiding. "Do not
seek to know it," said he; "you could not relieve it if you knew
it; you would not even seek to relieve it. On the contrary, I
should lose your sympathy, and that," said he, pressing my hand
convulsively, "that I feel has become too dear to me to risk."

I endeavored to awaken hope within him. He was young;
life had a thousand pleasures in store for him; there was a
healthy reaction in the youthful heart; it medicines [1] all its own
wounds. "Come, come," said I, "there is no grief so great that
youth cannot outgrow it." "No! no!" said he, clinching his
teeth, and striking repeatedly, with the energy of despair, on his
bosom, "it is here! here! deep rooted; draining my heart's blood.
It grows and grows, while my heart withers and withers. I have a
dreadful monitor that gives me no repose — that follows me step
by step — and will follow me step by step, until it pushes me into
my grave!"

As he said this he involuntarily gave one of those fearful
glances over his shoulder, and shrunk back with more than usual
horror. I could not resist the temptation to allude to this movement, which I supposed to be some mere malady of the nerves.
The moment I mentioned it, his face became crimsoned and
convulsed; he grasped me by both hands.

"For God's sake," exclaimed he, with a piercing voice, "never
allude to that again. Let us avoid this subject, my friend; you
cannot relieve me, — indeed you cannot relieve me, but you may
add to the torments I suffer. At some future day you shall
know all."

I never resumed the subject; for however much my curiosity
might be roused, I felt too true a compassion for his sufferings
to increase them by my intrusion. I sought various ways to
divert his mind, and to arouse him from the constant meditations
in which he was plunged. He saw my efforts, and seconded
them as far as was in his power, for there was nothing moody

[1] Cures.

or wayward in his nature. On the contrary, there was something frank, generous, unassuming, in his whole deportment. All the sentiments he uttered were noble and lofty. He claimed no indulgence, asked no toleration, but seemed content to carry his load of misery in silence, and only sought to carry it by my side. There was a mute, beseeching manner about him, as if he craved companionship as a charitable boon; and a tacit thankfulness in his looks, as if he felt grateful to me for not repulsing him.

I felt this melancholy to be infectious. It stole over my spirits, interfered with all my gay pursuits, and gradually saddened my life; yet I could not prevail upon myself to shake off a being who seemed to hang upon me for support. In truth, the generous traits of character which beamed through all his gloom penetrated to my heart. His bounty was lavish and open-handed; his charity, melting and spontaneous, not confined to mere donations, which humiliate as much as they relieve. The tone of his voice, the beam of his eye, enhanced every gift, and surprised the poor suppliant with that rarest and sweetest of charities, — the charity not merely of the hand, but of the heart. Indeed his liberality seemed to have something in it of self-abasement and expiation. He, in a manner, humbled himself before the mendicant. " What right have I to ease and affluence," would he murmur to himself, " when innocence wanders in misery and rags ? "

The carnival[1] time arrived. I hoped the gay scenes then presented might have some cheering effect. I mingled with him in the motley throng that crowded the Place of St. Mark. We frequented operas, masquerades, balls, — all in vain. The evil kept growing on him. He became more and more haggard and agitated. Often, after we had returned from one of these scenes of revelry, I have entered his room and found him lying on his face on the sofa, his hands clinched in his fine hair, and his whole countenance bearing traces of the convulsions of his mind.

The carnival passed away; the time of Lent succeeded; pas-

[1] A festival celebrated with merriment and revelry in Roman Catholic countries during the week before Lent.

6

sion week arrived. We attended one evening a solemn service in one of the churches, in the course of which a grand piece of vocal and instrumental music was performed relating to the death of our Savior.

I had remarked that he was always powerfully affected by music; on this occasion he was so in an extraordinary degree. As the pealing notes swelled through the lofty aisles, he seemed to kindle with fervor; his eyes rolled upwards, until nothing but the whites were visible; his hands were clasped together, until the fingers were deeply imprinted in the flesh. When the music expressed the dying agony, his face gradually sank upon his knees; and at the touching words resounding through the church, " *Gesu mori,*" [1] sobs burst from him uncontrolled. I had never seen him weep before. His had always been agony rather than sorrow. I augured well from the circumstance, and let him weep on uninterrupted. When the service was ended, we left the church. He hung on my arm as we walked homewards, with something of a softer and more subdued manner, instead of that nervous agitation I had been accustomed to witness. He alluded to the service we had heard. " Music," said he, " is indeed the voice of Heaven; never before have I felt more impressed by the story of the atonement of our Savior. — Yes, my friend," said he, clasping his hands with a kind of transport, " I know that my Redeemer liveth ! "

We parted for the night. His room was not far from mine, and I heard him for some time busied in it. I fell asleep, but was awakened before daylight. The young man stood by my bedside, dressed for traveling. He held a sealed packet and a large parcel in his hand, which he laid on the table.

" Farewell, my friend," said he, " I am about to set forth on a long journey; but, before I go I leave with you these remembrances. In this packet you will find the particulars of my story. When you read them I shall be far away. Do not remember me with aversion. You have been indeed a friend to me. You

---

[1] Jesus died.

have poured oil into a broken heart, but you could not heal it. Farewell! Let me kiss your hand — I am unworthy to embrace you." He sank on his knees, seized my hand in despite of my efforts to the contrary, and covered it with kisses. I was so surprised by all the scene that I had not been able to say a word. "But we shall meet again," said I, hastily, as I saw him hurrying towards the door. "Never, never, in this world !" said he, solemnly. He sprang once more to my bedside, seized my hand, pressed it to his heart and to his lips, and rushed out of the room.

Here the Baronet paused. He seemed lost in thought, and sat looking upon the floor, and drumming with his fingers on the arm of his chair.

"And did this mysterious personage return ? " said the inquisitive gentleman.

"Never ! " replied the Baronet, with a pensive shake of the head; "I never saw him again."

"And pray what has all this to do with the picture ? " inquired the old gentleman with the nose.

"True," said the questioner; "is it the portrait of that crack-brained Italian ? "

"No," said the Baronet dryly, not half liking the appellation given to his hero; "but this picture was inclosed in the parcel he left with me. The sealed packet contained its explanation. There was a request on the outside that I would not open it until six months had elapsed. I kept my promise in spite of my curiosity. I have a translation of it by me, and had meant to read it, by way of accounting for the mystery of the chamber; but I fear I have already detained the company too long."

Here there was a general wish expressed to have the manuscript read, particularly on the part of the inquisitive gentleman; so the worthy Baronet drew out a fairly written manuscript, and, wiping his spectacles, read aloud the following story:

THE STORY OF THE YOUNG ITALIAN.

I WAS born at Naples. My parents, though of noble rank, were limited in fortune, or rather, my father was ostentatious beyond his means, and expended so much on his palace, his equipage, and his retinue, that he was continually straitened in his pecuniary circumstances. I was a younger son, and looked upon with indifference by my father, who, from a principle of family pride, wished to leave all his property to my elder brother. I showed, when quite a child, an extreme sensibility. Everything affected me violently. While yet an infant in my mother's arms, and before I had learned to talk, I could be wrought upon to a wonderful degree of anguish or delight by the power of music. As I grew older, my feelings remained equally acute, and I was easily transported into paroxysms of pleasure or rage. It was the amusement of my relations and of the domestics to play upon [1] this irritable temperament. I was moved to tears, tickled to laughter, provoked to fury, for the entertainment of company, who were amused by such a tempest of mighty passion in a pigmy frame. They little thought, or perhaps little heeded, the dangerous sensibilities they were fostering. I thus became a little creature of passion before reason was developed. In a short time I grew too old to be a plaything, and then I became a torment. The tricks and passions I had been teased into became irksome, and I was disliked by my teachers for the very lessons they had taught me. My mother died; and my power as a spoiled child was at an end. There was no longer any necessity to humor or tolerate me, for there was nothing to be gained by it, as I was no favorite of my father. I therefore experienced the fate of a spoiled child in such a situation, and was neglected, or noticed only to be crossed and contradicted. Such was the early treatment of a heart which, if I can judge of

[1] " Play upon," i.e., make sport of.

it at all, was naturally disposed to the extremes of tenderness and affection.

My father, as I have already said, never liked me,—in fact, he never understood me; he looked upon me as willful and wayward, as deficient in natural affection. It was the stateliness of his own manner, the loftiness and grandeur of his own look, which had repelled me from his arms. I always pictured him to myself as I had seen him, clad in his senatorial robes, rustling with pomp and pride. The magnificence of his person daunted my young imagination. I could never approach him with the confiding affection of a child.

My father's feelings were wrapped up in my elder brother. He was to be the inheritor of the family title and the family dignity, and everything was sacrificed to him,—I, as well as everything else. It was determined to devote me to the Church, that so my humors and myself might be removed out of the way either of tasking my father's time and trouble, or interfering with the interests of my brother. At an early age, therefore, before my mind had dawned upon the world and its delights, or known anything of it beyond the precincts of my father's palace, I was sent to a convent, the superior of which was my uncle, and was confided entirely to his care.

My uncle was a man totally estranged from the world; he had never relished, for he had never tasted, its pleasures; and he regarded rigid self-denial as the great basis of Christian virtue. He considered every one's temperament like his own, or at least he made them conform to it. His character and habits had an influence over the fraternity of which he was superior; a more gloomy, saturnine set of beings were never assembled together. The convent, too, was calculated to awaken sad and solitary thoughts. It was situated in a gloomy gorge of those mountains away south of Vesuvius. All distant views were shut out by sterile volcanic heights. A mountain stream raved beneath its walls, and eagles screamed about its turrets.

I had been sent to this place at so tender an age as soon to lose all distinct recollection of the scenes I had left behind. As my mind expanded, therefore, it formed its idea of the world from the convent and its vicinity, and a dreary world it appeared to me. An early tinge of melancholy was thus infused into my character; and the dismal stories of the monks, about devils and evil spirits, with which they affrighted my young imagination, gave me a tendency to superstition which I could never effectually shake off. They took the same delight to work upon my ardent feelings, that had been so mischievously executed by my father's household. I can recollect the horrors with which they fed my heated fancy during an eruption of Vesuvius. We were distant from that volcano, with mountains between us; but its convulsive throes shook the solid foundations of nature. Earthquakes threatened to topple down our convent towers. A lurid, baleful light hung in the heavens at night, and showers of ashes, borne by the wind, fell in our narrow valley. The monks talked of the earth being honeycombed beneath us; of streams of molten lava raging through its veins; of caverns of sulphurous flames roaring in the center, the abodes of demons and the damned; of fiery gulfs ready to yawn beneath our feet. All these tales were told to the doleful accompaniment of the mountain's thunders, whose low bellowing made the walls of our convent vibrate.

One of the monks had been a painter, but had retired from the world, and embraced this dismal life in expiation of some crime. He was a melancholy man, who pursued his art in the solitude of his cell, but made it a source of penance to him. His employment was to portray, either on canvas or in waxen models, the human face and human form, in the agonies of death, and in all the stages of dissolution and decay. The fearful mysteries of the charnel house were unfolded in his labors; the loathsome banquet of the beetle and the worm. I turn with shuddering even from the recollection of his works; yet, at the time, my strong but ill-directed imagination seized with ardor upon his instructions in his art. Anything was a variety from the dry studies and monotonous duties of the cloister. In a lit-

tle while I became expert with my pencil, and my gloomy productions were thought worthy of decorating some of the altars
of the chapel.

In this dismal way was a creature of feeling and fancy brought
up. Everything genial and amiable in my nature was repressed,
and nothing brought out but what was unprofitable and ungra-
cious. I was ardent in my temperament ; quick, mercurial,[1] impetuous, formed to be a creature all love and adoration ; but a leaden
hand was laid on all my finer qualities. I was taught nothing
but fear and hatred. I hated my uncle ; I hated the monks ; I
hated the convent in which I was immured ; I hated the world ;
and I almost hated myself for being, as I supposed, so hating
and hateful an animal.

When I had nearly attained the age of sixteen, I was suffered,
on one occasion, to accompany one of the brethren on a mission
to a distant part of the country. We soon left behind us the
gloomy valley in which I had been pent up for so many years,
and after a short journey among the mountains, emerged upon
the voluptuous landscape that spreads itself about the Bay of
Naples. Heavens ! how transported was I when I stretched my
gaze over a vast reach of delicious sunny country, gay with
groves and vineyards ; with Vesuvius rearing its forked summit
to my right, the blue Mediterranean to my left, with its en-
chanting coast, studded with shining towns and sumptuous
villas, and Naples, my native Naples, gleaming far, far in the
distance.

Good God ! was this the lovely world from which I had been
excluded ! I had reached that age when the sensibilities are
in all their bloom and freshness. Mine had been checked and
chilled. They now burst forth with the suddenness of a re-
tarded springtime. My heart, hitherto unnaturally shrunk up,
expanded into a riot of vague but delicious emotions. The
beauty of nature intoxicated — bewildered me. The song of the
peasants, their cheerful looks, their happy avocations, the pic-

---

[1] Changeable.

turesque gayety of their dresses, their rustic music, their dances, —
all broke upon me like witchcraft. My soul responded to the
music, my heart danced in my bosom. All the men appeared
amiable, all the women lovely.

I returned to the convent, that is to say, my body returned,
but my heart and soul never entered there again. I could not
forget this glimpse of a beautiful and a happy world, — a world so
suited to my natural character. I had felt so happy while in it;
so different a being from what I felt myself when in the convent,
that tomb of the living. I contrasted the countenances of the beings I had seen, full of fire and freshness and enjoyment, with the
pallid, leaden, lackluster visages of the monks; the dance, with
the droning chant of the chapel. I had before found the exercises
of the cloister wearisome; they now became intolerable. The dull
round of duties wore away my spirit; my nerves became irri-
tated by the fretful tinkling of the convent bell, evermore ding-
ing among the mountain echoes, evermore calling me from my
repose at night, my pencil by day, to attend to some tedious and
mechanical ceremony of devotion.

I was not of a nature to meditate long without putting my
thoughts into action. My spirit had been suddenly aroused, and
was now all awake within me. I watched an opportunity, fled
from the convent, and made my way on foot to Naples. As I
entered its gay and crowded streets, and beheld the variety and
stir of life around me, the luxury of palaces, the splendor of
equipages, and the pantomimic animation of the motley populace, I seemed as if awakened to a world of enchantment, and
solemnly vowed that nothing should force me back to the monotony of the cloister.

I had to inquire my way to my father's palace, for I had been
so young on leaving it that I knew not its situation. I found
some difficulty in getting admitted to my father's presence; for
the domestics scarcely knew that there was such a being as myself in existence, and my monastic dress did not operate in my
favor. Even my father entertained no recollection of my per-

son. I told him my name, threw myself at his feet, implored his forgiveness, and entreated that I might not be sent back to the convent.

He received me with the condescension of a patron, rather than the fondness of a parent; listened patiently, but coldly, to my tale of monastic grievances and disgusts, and promised to think what else could be done for me. This coldness blighted and drove back all the frank affection of my nature, that was ready to spring forth at the least warmth of parental kindness. All my early feelings towards my father revived. I again looked up to him as the stately, magnificent being that had daunted my childish imagination, and felt as if I had no pretensions to his sympathies. My brother engrossed all his care and love; he inherited his nature, and carried himself towards me with a protecting rather than a fraternal air. It wounded my pride, which was great. I could brook condescension from my father, for I looked up to him with awe, as a superior being; but I could not brook patronage from a brother, who I felt was intellectually my inferior. The servants perceived that I was an unwelcome intruder in the paternal mansion, and, menial like, they treated me with neglect. Thus baffled at every point, my affections outraged wherever they would attach themselves, I became sullen, silent, and desponding. My feelings, driven back upon myself, entered and preyed upon my own heart. I remained for some days an unwelcome guest rather than a restored son in my father's house. I was doomed never to be properly known there. I was made, by wrong treatment, strange even to myself, and they judged of me from my strangeness.

I was startled one day at the sight of one of the monks of my convent gliding out of my father's room. He saw me, but pretended not to notice me, and this very hypocrisy made me suspect something. I had become sore and susceptible in my feelings; everything inflicted a wound on them. In this state of mind, I was treated with marked disrespect by a pampered minion, the favorite servant of my father. All the pride and passion

of my nature rose in an instant, and I struck him to the earth.
My father was passing by; he stopped not to inquire the reason,
nor indeed could he read the long course of mental sufferings
which were the real cause.   He rebuked me with anger and
scorn, summoning all the haughtiness of his nature and grandeur
of his look to give weight to the contumely with which he treated
me.   I felt that I had not deserved it.   I felt that I was not
appreciated.   I felt that I had that within me which merited
better treatment.   My heart swelled against a father's injustice.
I broke through my habitual awe of him; I replied to him with
impatience.   My hot spirit flushed in my cheek and kindled in
my eye; but my sensitive heart swelled as quickly, and before I
had half vented my passion, I felt it suffocated and quenched in
my tears.   My father was astonished and incensed at this turning of the worm, and ordered me to my chamber.   I retired in
silence, choking with contending emotions.

I had not been long there when I overheard voices in an
adjoining apartment.   It was a consultation between my father
and the monk, about the means of getting me back quietly to
the convent.   My resolution was taken.   I had no longer a home
nor a father.   That very night I left the paternal roof.   I got on
board a vessel about making sail from the harbor, and abandoned
myself to the wide world.   No matter to what port she steered;
any part of so beautiful a world was better than my convent.
No matter where I was cast by fortune; any place would be
more a home to me than the home I had left behind.   The vessel was bound to Genoa.   We arrived there after a voyage of a
few days.

As I entered the harbor between the moles which embrace it,
and beheld the amphitheater of palaces, and churches, and splen-
did gardens, rising one above another, I felt at once its title to
the appellation of "Genoa the Superb."   I landed on the mole,
an utter stranger, without knowing what to do, or whither to direct
my steps.   No matter; I was released from the thraldom of the
convent and the humiliations of home.   When I traversed the

Strada Balbi[1] and the Strada Nuova,[1] those streets of palaces, and gazed at the wonders of architecture around me; when I wandered at close of day amid a gay throng of the brilliant and the beautiful, through the green alleys of the Acquaverde,[2] or among the colonnades and terraces of the magnificent Doria gardens,[3] I thought it impossible to be ever otherwise than happy in Genoa. A few days sufficed to show me my mistake. My scanty purse was exhausted, and for the first time in my life I experienced the sordid distress of penury. I had never known the want of money, and had never adverted to the possibility of such an evil. I was ignorant of the world and all its ways; and when first the idea of destitution came over my mind, its effect was withering. I was wandering penniless through the streets which no longer delighted my eyes, when chance led my steps into the magnificent Church of the Annunciata.[4]

A celebrated painter of the day was at that moment superintending the placing of one of his pictures over an altar. The proficiency which I had acquired in his art during my residence in the convent, had made me an enthusiastic amateur. I was struck, at the first glance, with the painting. It was the face of a Madonna, so innocent, so lovely, such a divine expression of maternal tenderness! I lost, for the moment, all recollection of myself in the enthusiasm of my art. I clasped my hands together, and uttered an ejaculation of delight. The painter perceived my emotion. He was flattered and gratified by it. My air and manner pleased him, and he accosted me. I felt too much the want of friendship to repel the advances of a stranger;

[1] A fine street in the newer part of Genoa, containing palaces of superb architecture.

[2] The Piazza Acquaverde is a square in Genoa, now noted for the fine statue of Columbus, erected in 1862.

[3] The gardens of the Palace of Doria, presented to Andrea Doria, a Genoese statesman, in 1522. These gardens are very beautiful, and are famous for their fine orange trees.

[4] A church erected in 1487. In its interior it is the most magnificent in Genoa. The dome is richly decorated with works of art.

and there was something in this one so benevolent and winning, that in a moment he gained my confidence.

I told him my story and my situation, concealing only my name and rank. He appeared strongly interested by my recital, invited me to his house, and from that time I became his favorite pupil. He thought he perceived in me extraordinary talents for the art, and his encomiums awakened all my ardor. What a blissful period of my existence was it that I passed beneath his roof ! Another being seemed created within me, or rather, all that was amiable and excellent was drawn out. I was as recluse as ever I had been at the convent, but how different was my seclusion ! My time was spent in storing my mind with lofty and poetical ideas ; in meditating on all that was striking and noble in history and fiction ; in studying and tracing all that was sublime and beautiful in nature. I was always a visionary, imaginative being, but now my reveries and imaginings all elevated me to rapture. I looked up to my master as to a benevolent genius that had opened to me a region of enchantment. He was not a native of Genoa, but had been drawn thither by the solicitations of several of the nobility, and had resided there but a few years, for the completion of certain works. His health was delicate, and he had to confide much of the filling up of his designs to the pencils of his scholars. He considered me as particularly happy [1] in delineating the human countenance ; in seizing upon characteristic though fleeting expressions, and fixing them powerfully upon my canvas. I was employed continually, therefore, in sketching faces, and often, when some particular grace or beauty of expression was wanted in a countenance, it was intrusted to my pencil. My benefactor was fond of bringing me forward ; and partly, perhaps, through my actual skill, and partly through his partial praises, I began to be noted for the expressions of my countenances.

Among the various works which he had undertaken, was an historical piece for one of the palaces of Genoa, in which were

---

[1] Successful.

to be introduced the likenesses of several of the family. Among these was one intrusted to my pencil. It was that of a young girl, as yet in a convent for her education. She came out for the purpose of sitting for the picture. I first saw her in an apartment of one of the sumptuous palaces of Genoa. She stood before a casement that looked out upon the bay ; a stream of vernal sunshine fell upon her, and shed a kind of glory round her, as it lit up the rich crimson chamber. She was but sixteen years of age—and oh, how lovely ! The scene broke upon me like a mere vision of spring and youth and beauty. I could have fallen down and worshiped her. She was like one of those fictions of poets and painters, when they would express the *beau ideal* that haunts their minds with shapes of indescribable perfection. I was permitted to watch her countenance in various positions, and I fondly protracted the study that was undoing me. The more I gazed on her, the more I became enamored ; there was something almost painful in my intense admiration. I was but nineteen years of age, shy, diffident, and inexperienced. I was treated with attention by her mother ; for my youth and my enthusiasm in my art had won favor for me, and I am inclined to think something in my air and manner inspired interest and respect. Still the kindness with which I was treated could not dispel the embarrassment into which my own imagination threw me when in the presence of this lovely being. It elevated her into something almost more than mortal. She seemed too exquisite for earthly use, too delicate and exalted for human attainment. As I sat tracing her charms on my canvas, with my eyes occasionally riveted on her features, I drank in delicious poison that made me giddy. My heart alternately gushed with tenderness, and ached with despair. Now I became more than ever sensible of the violent fires that had lain dormant at the bottom of my soul. You who were born in a more temperate climate, and under a cooler sky, have little idea of the violence of passion in our southern bosoms.

A few days finished my task. Bianca returned to her convent, but her image remained indelibly impressed upon my heart. It dwelt in my imagination; it became my pervading idea of beauty. It had an effect even upon my pencil. I became noted for my felicity in depicting female loveliness. It was but because I multiplied the image of Bianca. I soothed and yet fed my fancy by introducing her in all the productions of my master. I have stood with delight in one of the chapels of the Annunciata, and heard the crowd extol the seraphic beauty of a saint which I had painted. I have seen them bow down in adoration before the painting. They were bowing before the loveliness of Bianca.

I existed in this kind of dream — I might almost say delirium — for upwards of a year. Such is the tenacity of my imagination, that the image formed in it continued in all its power and freshness. Indeed, I was a solitary, meditative being, much given to reverie, and apt to foster ideas which had once taken strong possession of me. I was roused from this fond, melancholy, delicious dream by the death of my worthy benefactor. I cannot describe the pangs his death occasioned me. It left me alone, and almost broken-hearted. He bequeathed to me his little property, which, from the liberality of his disposition, and his expensive style of living, was indeed but small; and he most particularly recommended me, in dying, to the protection of a nobleman who had been his patron.

The latter was a man who passed for munificent. He was a lover and an encourager of the arts, and evidently wished to be thought so. He fancied he saw in me indications of future excellence; my pencil had already attracted attention; he took me at once under his protection. Seeing that I was overwhelmed with grief, and incapable of exerting myself in the mansion of my late benefactor, he invited me to sojourn for a time at a villa which he possessed on the border of the sea, in the picturesque neighborhood of Sestri di Ponente.[1]

I found at the villa the count's only son, Filippo. He was near-

---

[1] A maritime town of Italy, four miles west of Genoa, having many country residences of the Genoese citizens.

ly of my age, prepossessing in his appearance, and fascinating in his manners; he attached himself to me, and seemed to court my good opinion. I thought there was something of profession in his kindness, and of caprice in his disposition; but I had nothing else near me to attach myself to, and my heart felt the need of something to repose upon. His education had been neglected; he looked upon me as his superior in mental powers and acquirements, and tacitly acknowledged my superiority. I felt that I was his equal in birth, and that gave independence to my manners, which had its effect. The caprice and tyranny I saw sometimes exercised on others over whom he had power, were never manifested towards me. We became intimate friends and frequent companions. Still, I loved to be alone, and to indulge in the reveries of my own imagination among the scenery by which I was surrounded. The villa commanded a wide view of the Mediterranean, and of the picturesque Ligurian coast.[1] It stood alone in the midst of ornamented grounds, finely decorated with statues and fountains, and laid out in groves and alleys and shady lawns. Everything was assembled here that could gratify the taste or agreeably occupy the mind. Soothed by the tranquillity of this elegant retreat, the turbulence of my feelings gradually subsided, and blending with the romantic spell which still reigned over my imagination, produced a soft, voluptuous melancholy.

I had not been long under the roof of the count when our solitude was enlivened by another inhabitant. It was a daughter of a relative of the count, who had lately died in reduced circumstances, bequeathing this only child to his protection. I had heard much of her beauty from Filippo, but my fancy had become so engrossed by one idea of beauty as not to admit of any other. We were in the central saloon of the villa when she arrived. She was still in mourning, and approached, leaning on the count's arm. As they ascended the marble portico, I was struck by the elegance of her figure and movement, by the grace

---

[1] Liguria, a mountainous region of Italy, comprising the provinces of Genoa and Porto Maurizio.

with which the *mezzaro*, the bewitching veil of Genoa, was folded about her slender form. They entered. Heavens ! what was my surprise when I beheld Bianca before me ! It was herself, pale with grief, but still more matured in loveliness than when I had last beheld her. The time that had elapsed had developed the graces of her person, and the sorrow she had undergone had diffused over her countenance an irresistible tenderness.

She blushed and trembled at seeing me, and tears rushed into her eyes, for she remembered in whose company she had been accustomed to behold me. For my part, I cannot express what were my emotions. By degrees I overcame the extreme shyness that had formerly paralyzed me in her presence. We were drawn together by sympathy of situation. We had each lost our best friend in the world ; we were each, in some measure, thrown upon the kindness of others. When I came to know her intellectually, all my ideal picturings of her were confirmed. Her newness to the world, her delightful susceptibility to everything beautiful and agreeable in nature, reminded me of my own emotions when first I escaped from the convent. Her rectitude of thinking delighted my judgment ; the sweetness of her nature wrapped itself round my heart ; and then her young, and tender, and budding loveliness sent a delicious madness to my brain.

I gazed upon her with a kind of idolatry, as something more than mortal ; and I felt humiliated at the idea of my comparative unworthiness. Yet she was mortal ; and one of mortality's most susceptible and loving compounds, — for she loved me !

How first I discovered the transporting truth I cannot recollect. I believe it stole upon me by degrees, as a wonder past hope or belief. We were both at such a tender and loving age, in constant intercourse with each other, mingling in the same elegant pursuits, for music, poetry, and painting were our mutual delights, and we were almost separated from society among lovely and romantic scenery. Is it strange that two young hearts thus brought together should readily twine round each other ?

O gods ! what a dream — a transient dream of unalloyed delight — then passed over my soul !   Then it was that the world
around me was indeed a paradise ; for I had woman — lovely,
delicious woman — to share it with me !   How often have I ram-
bled along the picturesque shores of Sestri, or climbed its wild
mountains, with the coast gemmed with villas, and the blue sea
far below me, and the slender Faro[1] of Genoa on its romantic
promontory[2] in the distance; and as I sustained the faltering
steps of Bianca, have thought there could no unhappiness enter into so beautiful a world !   How often have we listened
together to the nightingale, as it poured forth its rich notes
among the moonlight bowers of the garden, and have wondered
that poets could ever have fancied anything melancholy in its
song !   Why, oh why, is this budding season of life and tenderness so transient !   Why is this rosy cloud of love, that sheds
such a glow over the morning of our days, so prone to brew up
into the whirlwind and the storm !

I was the first to awaken from this blissful delirium of the affections.   I had gained Bianca's heart — what was I to do with it ?
I had no wealth nor prospect to entitle me to her hand.   Was I
to take advantage of her ignorance of the world, of her confiding affection, and draw her down to my own poverty ?   Was
this requiting the hospitality of the count ?   Was this requiting
the love of Bianca ?

Now first I began to feel that even successful love may have
its bitterness.   A corroding care gathered about my heart.   I
moved about the palace like a guilty being.   I felt as if I had
abused its hospitality, as if I were a thief within its walls.   I
could no longer look with unembarrassed mien in the countenance of the count.   I accused myself of perfidy to him, and I
thought he read it in my looks and began to distrust and despise
me.   His manner had always been ostentatious and condescend-

---

[1] The lighthouse of Genoa; a beautiful structure, three hundred feet high.
[2] Cape Faro, in the southern extremity of Genoa, on a slender piece of
land.

7

ing; it now appeared cold and haughty.   Filippo, too, became re-served and distant, or at least I suspected him to be so.   Heavens! was this the mere coinage of my brain ?   Was I to become sus-picious of all the world ? a poor, surmising wretch, watching looks and gestures, and torturing myself with misconstructions ?   Or, if true, was I to remain beneath a roof where I was merely tol-erated, and linger there on sufferance ?   " This is not to be en-dured !" exclaimed I.   " I will tear myself from this state of self-abasement; I will break through this fascination, and fly — Fly! — whither ? from the world? for where-is the world when I leave Bianca behind me ? "

My spirit was naturally proud, and swelled within me at the idea of being looked upon with contumely.   Many times I was on the point of declaring my family and rank, and asserting my equality in the presence of Bianca, when I thought her relations assumed an air of superiority.   But the feeling was transient.   I considered myself discarded and condemned by my family, and had solemnly vowed never to own relationship to them until they themselves should claim it.

The struggle of my mind preyed upon my happiness and my health.   It seemed as if the uncertainty of being loved would be less intolerable than thus to be assured of it, and yet not dare to enjoy the conviction.   I was no longer the enraptured admirer of Bianca ; I no longer hung in ecstasy on the tones of her voice, nor drank in with insatiate gaze the beauty of her countenance. Her very smiles ceased to delight me, for I felt culpable in hav-ing won them.

She could not but be sensible of the change in me, and inquired the cause with her usual frankness and simplicity.   I could not evade the inquiry, for my heart was full to aching.   I told her all the conflict of my soul, my devouring passion, my bitter self-upbraiding.   " Yes," said I, " I am unworthy of you.   I am an offcast from my family, — a wanderer, — a nameless, homeless wanderer, with nothing but poverty for my portion ; and yet I have dared to love you — have dared to aspire to your love."

My agitation moved her to tears, but she saw nothing in my situation so hopeless as I had depicted it. Brought up in a convent, she knew nothing of the world, — its wants, its cares ; and indeed, what woman is a worldly casuist in the matters of the heart ? Nay, more, she kindled into sweet enthusiasm when she spoke of my fortunes and myself. We had dwelt together on the works of the famous masters. I related to her their histories, the high reputation, the influence, the magnificence to which they had attained, — the companions of princes, the favorites of kings, the pride and boast of nations. All this she applied to me. Her love saw nothing in all their great productions that I was not able to achieve ; and when I beheld the lovely creature glow with fervor, and her whole countenance radiant with visions of my glory, I was snatched up for the moment into the heaven of her own imagination.

I am dwelling too long upon this part of my story, yet I cannot help lingering over a period of my life on which, with all its cares and conflicts, I look back with fondness, for as yet my soul was unstained by a crime. I do not know what might have been the result of this struggle between pride, delicacy, and passion, had I not read in a Neapolitan gazette an account of the sudden death of my brother. It was accompanied by an earnest inquiry for intelligence concerning me, and a prayer, should this meet my eye, that I would hasten to Naples to comfort an infirm and afflicted father.

I was naturally of an affectionate disposition, but my brother had never been as a brother to me. I had long considered myself as disconnected from him, and his death caused me but little emotion. The thoughts of my father, infirm and suffering, touched me, however, to the quick, and when I thought of him, that lofty, magnificent being, now bowed down and desolate, and suing to me for comfort, all my resentment for past neglect was subdued, and a glow of filial affection was awakened within me.

The predominant feeling, however, that overpowered all others, was transport at the sudden change in my whole fortunes. A home, a name, rank, wealth, awaited me; and love painted a still more rapturous prospect in the distance. I hastened to Bianca, and threw myself at her feet. " O Bianca !" exclaimed I, " at length I can claim you for my own. I am no longer a nameless adventurer, a neglected, rejected outcast. Look — read — behold the tidings that restore me to my name and to myself ! "

I will not dwell on the scene that ensued. Bianca rejoiced in the reverse of my situation, because she saw it lightened my heart of a load of care; for her own part, she had loved me for myself, and had never doubted that my own merits would command both fame and fortune.

I now felt all my native pride buoyant within me. I no longer walked with my eyes bent to the dust; hope elevated them to the skies; my soul was lit up with fresh fires, and beamed from my countenance.

I wished to impart the change in my circumstances to the count, to let him know who and what I was, and to make formal proposals for the hand of Bianca; but he was absent on a distant estate. I opened my whole soul to Filippo. Now first I told him of my passion, of the doubts and fears that had distracted me, and of the tidings that had suddenly dispelled them. He overwhelmed me with congratulations, and with the warmest expressions of sympathy. I embraced him in the fullness of my heart; I felt compunctious for having suspected him of coldness, and asked his forgiveness for ever having doubted his friendship.

Nothing is so warm and enthusiastic as a sudden expansion of the heart between young men. Filippo entered into our concerns with the most eager interest. He was our confidant and counselor. It was determined that I should hasten at once to Naples, to reëstablish myself in my father's affections and my paternal home; and the moment the reconciliation was effected, and my father's consent insured, I should return and demand Bianca of the count. Filippo engaged to secure his father's acquiescence; indeed he undertook to watch over our interest, and to be the channel through which we might correspond.

My parting with Bianca was tender, delicious, agonizing. It was in a little pavilion of the garden which had been one of our favorite resorts. How often and often did I return to have one more adieu; to have her look once more on me in speechless emotion; to enjoy once more the rapturous sight of those tears streaming down her lovely cheeks; to seize once more on that delicate hand, the frankly accorded pledge of love, and cover it with tears and kisses! Heavens! there is a delight even in the parting agony of two lovers worth a thousand tame pleasures of the world. I have her at this moment before my eyes, at the window of the pavilion, putting aside the vines which clustered about the casement, her form beaming forth in virgin light, her countenance all tears and smiles, sending a thousand and a thousand adieus after me, as, hesitating in a delirium of fondness and agitation, I faltered my way down the avenue.

As the bark bore me out of the harbor of Genoa, how eagerly my eye stretched along the coast of Sestri till it discovered the villa gleaming from among the trees at the foot of the mountain. As long as day lasted I gazed and gazed upon it, till it lessened and lessened to a mere white speck in the distance; and still my intense and fixed gaze discerned it, when all other objects of the coast had blended into indistinct confusion, or were lost in the evening gloom.

On arriving at Naples, I hastened to my paternal home. My heart yearned for the long withheld blessing of a father's love. As I entered the proud portal of the ancestral palace, my emotions were so great that I could not speak. No one knew me; the servants gazed at me with curiosity and surprise. A few years of intellectual elevation and development had made a prodigious change in the poor fugitive stripling from the convent. Still, that no one should know me in my rightful home was overpowering. I felt like the prodigal son returned. I was a stranger in the house of my father. I burst into tears and wept aloud.

When I made myself known, however, all was changed. I, who had once been almost repulsed from its walls, and forced to fly as an exile, was welcomed back with acclamation, with servility. One of the servants hastened to prepare my father for my reception. My eagerness to receive the paternal embrace was so great that I could not await his return, but hurried after him. What a spectacle met my eyes as I entered the chamber! My father, whom I had left in the pride of vigorous age, whose noble and majestic bearing had so awed my young imagination, was bowed down and withered into decrepitude. A paralysis had ravaged his stately form, and left it a shaking ruin. He sat propped up in his chair, with pale, relaxed visage, and glassy, wandering eye. His intellect had evidently shared in the ravages of his frame. The servant was endeavoring to make him comprehend that a visitor was at hand. I tottered up to him, and sank at his feet. All his past coldness and neglect were forgotten in his present sufferings. I remembered only that he was my parent, and that I had deserted him. I clasped his knee; my voice was almost filled with convulsive sobs. " Pardon—pardon! O my father!" was all that I could utter. His apprehension seemed slowly to return to him. He gazed at me for some moments with a vague, inquiring look, a convulsive tremor quivered about his lips, he feebly extended a shaking hand, laid it upon my head, and burst into an infantine flow of tears.

From that moment he would scarcely spare me from his sight. I appeared the only object that his heart responded to in the world; all else was as a blank to him. He had almost lost the power of speech, and the reasoning faculty seemed at an end. He was mute and passive, excepting that fits of childlike weeping would sometimes come over him without any immediate cause. If I left the room at any time, his eye was incessantly fixed on the door till my return, and on my entrance there was another gush of tears.

To talk with him of all my concerns, in this ruined state of mind, would have been worse than useless; to have left him for ever so short a time would have been cruel, unnatural. Here, then, was a new trial for my affections. I wrote to Bianca an account of my return, and of my actual situation, painting in colors vivid, for they were true, the torments I suffered at our being thus separated; for the youthful lover every day of absence is an age of love lost. I inclosed the letter in one to Filippo, who was the channel of our correspondence. I received a reply from him full of friendship and sympathy, from Bianca, full of assurances of affection and constancy. Week after week, month after month elapsed without making any change in my circumstances. The vital flame which had seemed nearly extinct when first I met my father, kept fluttering on without any apparent diminution. I watched him constantly, faithfully, I had almost said patiently. I knew that his death alone would set me free, yet I never at any moment wished it. I felt too glad to be able to make any atonement for past disobedience; and denied, as I had been, all endearments of relationship in my early days, my heart yearned towards a father who in his age and helplessness had thrown himself entirely on me for comfort.

My passion for Bianca gained daily more force from absence; by constant meditation it wore itself a deeper and deeper channel. I made no new friends nor acquaintances, sought none of the pleasures of Naples which my rank and fortune threw open to me. Mine was a heart that confined itself to few objects, but dwelt upon them with the intenser passion. To sit by my father, administer to his wants, and to meditate on Bianca in the silence of his chamber, was my constant habit. Sometimes I amused myself with my pencil in portraying the image ever present to my imagination. I transferred to canvas every look and smile of hers that dwelt in my heart. I showed them to my father, in hopes of awakening an interest in his bosom for the mere shadow of my love; but he was too far sunk in intellect to take any notice of them. When I received a letter from Bianca, it was a new source of solitary luxury. Her letters, it is true, were less and less frequent, but they were always full of assurances of unabated affection. They breathed not the frank and innocent warmth with which she expressed herself in conversation, but I accounted for it from the embarrassment which inexperienced minds have often to express themselves upon paper. Filippo assured me of her unaltered constancy. They both lamented, in the strongest terms, our continued separation, though they did justice to the filial piety that kept me by my father's side.

Nearly two years elapsed in this protracted exile. To me they were so many ages. Ardent and impetuous by nature, I scarcely know how I should have supported so long an absence had I not felt assured that the faith of Bianca was equal to my own. At length my father died. Life went from him almost imperceptibly. I hung over him in mute affliction, and watched the expiring spasms of nature. His last faltering accents whispered repeatedly a blessing on me. Alas! how has it been fulfilled!

When I had paid due honors to his remains, and laid them in the tomb of our ancestors, I arranged briefly my affairs, put them in a posture to be easily at my command from a distance, and embarked once more with a bounding heart for Genoa.

Our voyage was propitious, and oh, what was my rapture when first, in the dawn of morning, I saw the shadowy summits of the Apennines rising almost like clouds above the horizon! The sweet breath of summer just moved us over the long wavering billows that were rolling us on towards Genoa. By degrees the coast of Sestri rose like a creation of enchantment from the silver bosom of the deep. I beheld the line of villages and palaces studding its borders. My eye reverted to a well-known point, and at length, from the confusion of distant objects, it singled out the villa which contained Bianca. It was a mere speck in the landscape, but glimmering from afar, the polar star of my heart.

Again I gazed at it for a livelong summer's day, but oh, how different the emotions between departure and return! It now kept growing and growing, instead of lessening and lessening, on my sight. My heart seemed to dilate with it. I looked at it through a telescope. I gradually defined one feature after another. The balconies of the second saloon where first I met Bianca beneath its roof; the terrace where we so often had passed the delightful summer evenings; the awning which shaded her chamber window; I almost fancied I saw her form beneath it. Could she but know her lover was in the bark whose white sail now gleamed on the sunny bosom of the sea ! My fond impatience increased as we neared the coast; the ship seemed to lag lazily over the billows; I could almost have sprung into the sea, and swum to the desired shore.

The shadows of evening gradually shrouded the scene, but the moon arose in all her fullness and beauty, and shed the tender light so dear to lovers over the romantic coast of Sestri. My soul was bathed in unutterable tenderness. I anticipated the heavenly evenings I should pass in once more wandering with Bianca by the light of that blessed moon.

It was late at night before we entered the harbor. As early next morning as I could get released from the formalities of landing, I threw myself on horseback, and hastened to the villa. As I galloped round the rocky promontory on which stands the Faro, and saw the coast of Sestri opening upon me, a thousand anxieties and doubts suddenly sprang up in my bosom. There is something fearful in returning to those we love, while yet uncertain what ills or changes absence may have effected. The turbulence of my agitation shook my very frame. I spurred my horse to redoubled speed; he was covered with foam when we both arrived panting at the gateway that opened to the grounds around the villa. I left my horse at a cottage, and walked through the grounds, that I might regain tranquillity for the approaching interview. I chid myself for having suffered mere doubts and surmises thus suddenly to overcome me; but I was always prone to be carried away by gusts of the feelings.

On entering the garden, everything bore the same look as when I had left it; and this unchanged aspect of things reassured me. There were the alleys in which I had so often walked with Bianca, as we listened to the song of the nightingale; the same shades under which we had so often sat during the noontide heat. There were the same flowers of which she was so fond, and which appeared still to be under the ministry of her hand. Everything looked and breathed of Bianca; hope and joy flushed in my bosom at every step. I passed a little arbor, in which we had often sat and read together; a book and glove lay on the bench; it was Bianca's glove; it was a volume of the "Metastasio"[1] I had given her. The glove lay in my favorite passage. I clasped them to my heart with rapture. "All is safe!" exclaimed I; "she loves me, she is still my own!"

I bounded lightly along the avenue down which I had faltered slowly at my departure. I beheld her favorite pavilion, which had witnessed our parting scene. The window was open, with the same vine clambering about it, precisely as when she waved and wept me an adieu. Oh, how transporting was the contrast in my situation! As I passed near the pavilion, I heard the tones of a female voice; they thrilled through me with an appeal to my heart not to be mistaken. Before I could think, I *felt* they were Bianca's. For an instant I paused, overpowered with agitation. I feared to break so suddenly upon her. I softly ascended the steps of the pavilion. The door was open. I saw Bianca seated at a table; her back was towards me; she was warbling a soft, melancholy air, and was occupied in drawing. A glance sufficed to show me that she was copying one of my own paintings. I gazed on her for a moment in a delicious tumult of emotions. She paused in her singing: a heavy sigh, almost a sob, followed. I could no longer contain myself. "Bianca!" exclaimed I, in a half-smothered voice. She started at the sound, brushed back the ringlets that hung clustering about her face, darted a glance at me, uttered a piercing shriek, and would have fallen to the earth had I not caught her in my arms.

---

[1] A famous Italian poet (1698–1782). His real name was Trapassi, which was changed to Metastasio ("a changing") on his adoption by the jurist Gravina.

" Bianca ! my own Bianca !" exclaimed I, folding her to my
bosom, my voice stifled in sobs of convulsive joy. She lay in
my arms without sense or motion. Alarmed at the effects of my
precipitation, I scarce knew what to do. I tried by a thousand
endearing words to call her back to consciousness. She slowly
recovered, and half opened her eyes. "Where am I ? " murmured she faintly. "Here !" exclaimed I, pressing her to my
bosom, "here — close to the heart that adores you — in the arms
of your faithful Ottavio !" "Oh, no ! no ! no !" shrieked she,
starting into sudden life and terror. "Away ! away ! leave me !
leave me !"

She tore herself from my arms, rushed to a corner of the
saloon, and covered her face with her hands, as if the very sight
of me were baleful. I was thunderstruck. I could not believe
my senses. I followed her, trembling, confounded. I endeavored
to take her hand, but she shrunk from my very touch with horror.

" Good heavens, Bianca !" exclaimed I, "what is the meaning
of this ? Is this my reception after so long an absence ? Is
this the love you professed for me ? "

At the mention of love, a shuddering ran through her. She
turned to me a face wild with anguish. "No more of that — no
more of that !" gasped she; "talk not to me of love! I—I—
am married !"

I reeled as if I had received a mortal blow ; a sickness struck
to my very heart. I caught at a window frame for support.
For a moment or two everything was chaos around me. When
I recovered, I beheld Bianca lying on a sofa, her face buried in
the pillow, and sobbing convulsively. Indignation for her fickle-
ness for a moment overpowered every other feeling.

" Faithless ! perjured !" cried I, striding across the room. But
another glance at that beautiful being in distress checked all my
wrath. Anger could not dwell together with her idea in my soul.

" Oh, Bianca !" exclaimed I, in anguish, "could I have dreamed
of this ? Could I have suspected you would have been false to
me ? "

She raised her face, all streaming with tears, all disordered with emotion, and gave me one appealing look. "False to you? They told me you were dead!"

"What!" said I, "in spite of our constant correspondence?"

She gazed wildly at me. "Correspondence? what correspondence?"

"Have you not repeatedly received and replied to my letters?"

She clasped her hands with solemnity and fervor. "As I hope for mercy—never!"

A horrible surmise shot through my brain. "Who told you I was dead?"

"It was reported that the ship in which you embarked for Naples perished at sea."

"But who told you the report?"

She paused for an instant, and trembled;—"Filippo!"

"May the God of heaven curse him!" cried I, extending my clinched fists aloft.

"Oh, do not curse him, do not curse him!" exclaimed she; "he is—he is—my husband!"

This was all that was wanting to unfold the perfidy that had been practiced upon me. My blood boiled like liquid fire in my veins. I gasped with rage too great for utterance. I remained for a time bewildered by the whirl of horrible thoughts that rushed through my mind. The poor victim of deception before me thought it was with her I was incensed. She faintly murmured forth her exculpation. I will not dwell upon it. I saw in it more than she meant to reveal. I saw with a glance how both of us had been betrayed.

"'Tis well," muttered I to myself in smothered accents of concentrated fury. "He shall render an account of all this."

Bianca overheard me. New terror flashed in her countenance. "For mercy's sake, do not meet him! say nothing of what has passed—for my sake say nothing to him. I only shall be the sufferer!"

A new suspicion darted across my mind. "What!" exclaimed

I, "do you then *fear* him ? Is he *unkind* to you ? Tell me," reiterated I, grasping her hand, and looking her eagerly in the face, "tell me—*dares* he to use you harshly ? "

" No, no, no !" cried she, faltering and embarrassed; but the glance at her face had told volumes. I saw in her pallid and wasted features, in the prompt terror and subdued agony of her eye, a whole history of a mind broken down by tyranny. Great God ! and was this beauteous flower snatched from me to be thus trampled upon ? The idea roused me to madness. I clinched my teeth and hands ; I foamed at the mouth ; every passion seemed to have resolved itself into the fury that like a lava boiled within my heart. Bianca shrunk from me in speechless affright. As I strode by the window, my eye darted down the alley. Fatal moment ! I beheld Filippo at a distance. My brain was in delirium. I sprang from the pavilion, and was before him with the quickness of lightning. He saw me as I came rushing upon him ; he turned pale, looked wildly to right and left, as if he would have fled, and trembling, drew his sword.

"Wretch !" cried I, "well may you draw your weapon !"

I spoke not another word. I snatched forth a stiletto, put by the sword which trembled in his hand, and buried my poniard in his bosom. He fell with the blow, but my rage was unsated. I sprang upon him with the bloodthirsty feeling of a tiger, redoubled my blows, mangled him in my frenzy, grasped him by the throat, until, with reiterated wounds and strangling convulsions, he expired in my grasp. I remained glaring on the countenance, horrible in death, that seemed to stare back with its protruded eyes upon me. Piercing shrieks roused me from my delirium. I looked round and beheld Bianca flying distractedly towards us. My brain whirled; I waited not to meet her, but fled from the scene of horror. I fled forth from the garden like another Cain, a hell within my bosom, and a curse upon my head. I fled without knowing whither, almost without knowing why. My only idea was to get farther and farther from the horrors I had left behind—as if I could throw space between myself and my conscience. I fled to the Apennines, and wandered for days and days among their savage heights. How I existed I cannot tell; what rocks and precipices I braved, and how I braved them, I know not. I kept on and on, trying to outtravel the curse that clung to me. Alas! the shrieks of Bianca rung forever in my ears. The horrible countenance of my victim was forever before my eyes. The blood of Filippo cried to me from the ground. Rocks, trees, and torrents, all resounded with my crime. Then it was I felt how much more insupportable is the anguish of remorse than every other mental pang. Oh, could I but have cast off this crime that festered in my heart! Could I but have regained the innocence that reigned in my breast as I entered the garden at Sestri! Could I but have restored my victim to life, I felt as if I could look on with transport, even though Bianca were in his arms.

By degrees this frenzied fever of remorse settled into a permanent malady of the mind, — into one of the most horrible that ever poor wretch was cursed with. Wherever I went, the countenance of him I had slain appeared to follow me. Whenever I turned my head, I beheld it behind me, hideous with the contortions of the dying moment. I have tried in every way to escape from this horrible phantom, but in vain. I know not whether it be an illusion of the mind, the consequence of my dismal education at the convent, or whether a phantom really sent by Heaven to punish me, but there it ever is, at all times, in all places. Nor has time nor habit had any effect in familiarizing me with its terrors. I have traveled from place to place, plunged into amusements, tried dissipation and distraction of every kind; all, all in vain. I once had recourse to my pencil as a desperate experiment. I painted an exact resemblance of this phantom face. I placed it before me, in hopes that by constantly contemplating the copy I might diminish the effect of the original. But I only doubled instead of diminishing the misery. Such is the curse that has clung to my footsteps; that has made my life a burden, but the thought of death terrible.

God knows what I have suffered,—what days and days, and nights and nights, of sleepless torment; what a never-dying worm has preyed upon my heart; what an unquenchable fire has burned within my brain !   He knows the wrongs that wrought upon my poor, weak nature; that converted the tenderest of affections into the deadliest of fury.   He knows best whether a frail, erring creature has expiated by long-enduring torture and measureless remorse the crime of a moment of madness.   Often, often, have I prostrated myself in the dust, and implored that He would give me a sign of his forgiveness, and let me die——

Thus far had I written some time since.   I had meant to leave this record of misery and crime with you, to be read when I should be no more.

My prayer to Heaven has at length been heard.   You were witness to my emotions last evening at the church, when the vaulted temple resounded with the words of atonement and re-demption.   I heard a voice speaking to me from the midst of the music; I heard it rising above the pealing of the organ and the voices of the choir; it spoke to me in tones of celestial melody; it promised mercy and forgiveness, but demanded from me full expiation.   I go to make it.   To-morrow I shall be on my way to Genoa, to surrender myself to justice.   You who have pitied my sufferings, who have poured the balm of sympathy into my wounds, do not shrink from my memory with abhorrence now that you know my story.   Recollect that when you read of my crime I shall have atoned for it with my blood !

When the Baronet had finished, there was a universal desire expressed to see the painting of this frightful visage.   After much entreaty, the Baronet consented on condition that they should only visit it one by one.   He called his housekeeper, and gave her charge to conduct the gentlemen, singly, to the chamber.   They all returned varying in their stories, some affected in one way, some in another, some more, some less, but all agreeing that there was a certain something about the painting that had a very odd effect upon the feelings.

I stood in a deep bow window with the Baronet, and could not help expressing my wonder. "After all," said I, "there are certain mysteries in our nature, certain inscrutable impulses and influences, which warrant one in being superstitious. Who can account for so many persons of different characters being thus strangely affected by a mere painting?"

"And especially when not one of them has seen it," said the Baronet, with a smile.

"How!" exclaimed I, "not seen it?"

"Not one of them!" replied he, laying his finger on his lips, in sign of secrecy. "I saw that some of them were in a bantering vein, and did not choose that the memento of the poor Italian should be made a jest of. So I gave the housekeeper a hint to show them all to a different chamber!"

Thus end the stories of the Nervous Gentleman.